M000209766

PRAYER and the KNOWLEDGE of GOD

What the Whole Bible Teaches

GRAEME GOLDSWORTHY

IVP Books
An imprint of InterVarsity Press
Downers Grove, Illinois

InterVarsity Press
P.O. Box 1400, Downers Grove, IL 60515-1426
Internet: www.ivpress.com
E-mail: email@ivpress.com

Published in the United States of America by InterVarsity Press, Downers Grove, Illinois, with permission from Inter-Varsity Press, Leicester, England.

InterVarsity Press® is the book-publishing division of InterVarsity Christian Fellowship/USA®, a movement of students and faculty active on campus at hundreds of universities, colleges and schools of nursing in the United States of America, and a member movement of the International Fellowship of Evangelical Students. For information about local and regional activities, write Public Relations Dept., InterVarsity Christian Fellowship/USA, 6400 Schroeder Rd., P.O. Box 7895, Madison, WI 53707-7895, or visit the IVCF website at <www.intervarsity.org>.

ISBN 978-0-8308-5366-3

Printed in the United States of America ∞

green press INITIATIVE *InterVarsity Press is committed to protecting the environment and to the responsible use of natural resources. As a member of the Green Press Initiative we use recycled paper whenever possible. To learn more about the Green Press Initiative, visit <www.greenpressinitiative.org>.*

Library of Congress Cataloging-in-Publication Data
A catalog record for this book is available from the Library of Congress.

P 25 24 23 22 21 20 19 18 17 16 15 14 13 12 11 10 9 8 7
Y 30 29 28 27 26 25 24 23 22 21 20 19 18 17 16 15 14 13

Contents

Preface

P. T. Forsyth begins his book, *The Soul of Prayer*, thus:

> It is a difficult and even formidable thing to write on prayer, and one fears to touch the Ark. Perhaps no one ought to undertake it unless he has spent more toil in the practice of prayer than on its principle. But perhaps also the effort to look into its principle may be graciously regarded by Him who ever liveth to make intercession as itself a prayer to know better how to pray. All progress in prayer is an answer to prayer – our own or another's. And all true prayer promotes its own progress and increases our power to pray.[1]

These are sobering thoughts for one who, perhaps rashly, here endeavours to understand better this subject, and I plead only the justification of my failures through the intercession of Christ. I know that, on Forsyth's criteria, I hardly qualify to undertake this study. There is, furthermore, a fairly extensive literature on the subject of prayer and one may well question the need for more. Because prayer is such a practical issue, it is not surprising that most of the literature is of a practical nature. While I certainly hope this book will be ultimately practical, I suspect that a lot of the works produced that are of a practical nature are fairly pragmatic and experience-based.

1. P. T. Forsyth, *The Soul of Prayer* (London: Charles H. Kelly, 1916), p. 9.

Pragmatism seeks what apparently works, often at the expense of seeking the basis for the valid judgment of what success or failure is. To base practice on experience is of course what we do all the time, but this too can be a diversion into a realm of superficiality if we lack the criteria for assessing the value of experience.

I write from the deep conviction and perspective of evangelical belief in the supreme authority of the Bible as God's word written. I have undertaken the task because I believe that the often-neglected method of biblical theology has much to offer us in the insights it can provide into the biblical teaching on prayer. As an evangelical I believe that pragmatism is an insidious threat to biblical Christianity. If things appear to be going well, we often take this as a sign that we are doing it right. We are all adept at accepting the rules, practices and spiritual clichés of our immediate sub-culture, be it of the local church, our denomination, or the para-church organization we identify with. We accept these notions from our elders and peers, often without question. These people are our spiritual mentors, and we stand with them in a venerable tradition of vibrant Christian faith. How can it be wrong in any significant way? In taking this stance we ignore one of the insights of the Reformation that the reformed church is always reforming. Enthusiasm without understanding is a deadly recipe for error. Consequently, we must be careful to be continually testing our beliefs and practices against the rule of Scripture.

This study began as some sermons in the local church and a theological college chapel, and as a series of studies prepared for weekend teaching schools in some local churches. My concern is both practical and foundational. Good practice comes from a sound understanding of the teaching of the Bible. Hence, the basic approach I take is the application of biblical theology within the framework of systematic theology. My aim is to get behind the practical questions that are so often raised in sermons, addresses and books on prayer. I have tried to understand something of the reality of God, the ministry of Jesus Christ, and our experience of being his redeemed people as the grounds for prayer.

I am grateful to those who encouraged me, some without realizing it, to complete this study. Anne Milton, assistant registrar of Moore Theological College, read the manuscript and offered valuable comments and suggestions. I want also to acknowledge the helpful evaluation and comments by Philip Duce, the editor, and to express my gratitude for the willingness of Inter-Varsity Press to publish the book.

Graeme Goldsworthy

1 Praying and its problems

Problems people have with prayer

A recent television report commented on a survey of hospital patients who had been prayed for, some of them without knowing it. These were compared with other sick people who had not been prayed for. The claim was made that those who had been prayed for showed quicker and better recoveries than the others. Although it was granted that proper controls for such a survey would be difficult, it was still suggested that prayer did make a difference. An unbeliever asked to comment saw the whole exercise and the claimed results as immoral. He said he could not believe in a God that so favoured the few who happened to have prayer support. One could understand the reaction, but it was also clear that the matter only served to reinforce some rather unbiblical notions of God in this man's mind. He seemed to think that Christians believed in a God who could be persuaded to favour certain people on the basis of prayer. Very often when a Christian is confronted with the 'I can't believe in a god who . . .' argument, the appropriate answer is, 'I don't believe in that god either.' This incident illustrates the need to consider prayer together with what it means to know God and to have fellowship with him.

Unbelievers are not the only ones who have problems with prayer. Most Christians to whom I have spoken about prayer have expressed various problems that they experience with it. That we *should* pray is a proposition readily agreed to. That we *may* pray is acknowledged as a great privilege belonging to the people of God. That most people find it difficult would seem to be the case, although the exact nature of the difficulties probably covers a wide range of things. Often the difficulty is related to a particular circumstance, but other problems are of a more general nature.

Perhaps you can identify with one or more of these statements:

> 'I sometimes feel my prayers don't go past the ceiling.'
> 'Why ask God for things that he knows we need anyway?'
> 'What's the point in praying if everything has been determined beforehand?'
> 'I can't keep my mind from wandering when I try to pray.'
> 'Can we really change God's mind?'
> 'My prayers seem like a lot of repetition and simply lack life.'
> 'Does God answer everyone's prayers?'
> 'Does it matter which person of the Trinity I pray to?'

We could go on adding to this list, but I imagine you get the point: some have problems with the actual practice of praying, while others wonder about the meaning of it as a part of living as a Christian. It is my belief that a lot of problems in actually getting down to praying stem from a lack of understanding of how prayer is possible, and about what is really going on when we pray. How, for example, does prayer fit into the overall scheme of things? There are, of course, the practical issues of self-discipline, laziness, being too busy, and so on. My experience is that much of the literature on the subject is aimed at urging us to be more constant in prayer. The same could be said of many of the sermons preached on the subject. Let me say that there is no doubt in my mind that meaningful prayer is a worthy goal, and I sincerely hope this book will contribute to the achieving of this goal.

The appeal to the godly example

The strategy of some writers and preachers in seeking to encourage Christians towards the desired goal is not always as helpful as its exponents seem to think. A popular approach is the mainly exemplary one, focusing on the examples set by the great biblical heroes of faith, especially Jesus, as those who knew how vital it is to pray, usually without much analysis of the basis for the whole practice of prayer. Examples are also drawn from Christian biography, and the sermons and books that focus on this approach are liberally seasoned with memorable quotes about the importance of prayer. Unfortunately, being told that Jesus got up a great while before sunrise in order to pray, or that Martin Luther, John Wesley and C.H. Spurgeon all regarded two hours a day spent in prayer as normal, does not seem to help most of us. On the contrary, it often tends to make us want to give up altogether. We simply find it too hard to even contemplate such discipline in the midst of our modern busy lives.

One of the problems associated with the exemplary approach is that it often lifts the example, biblical or otherwise, out of its own historical context. This may or may not affect the value of the example but, in the case of the biblical heroes, it also lifts them out of the context of what God was specifically doing in the history of redemption. It assumes that we can evaluate the example apart from its specific context. It has been wisely said that a biblical description is not a prescription. Great care is needed so that we do not simply argue that, since what a certain biblical character did was good, we must do the same in every detail. Examples are valuable for illustrating principles that are grounded on firmer foundations than such examples alone. They help us see the human element and the impact that certain principles can have in people's lives, without necessarily prescribing the way the principle should be applied in our own lives.

Why do we sometimes find these biblical and more modern examples to be so demoralizing? It is not simply that such a lifestyle seems unattainable in the midst of the multitude of daily tasks we need to perform as part of our hectic modern existence. We know that each of us has to seek to be responsible before God in ordering our daily life so that fellowship with him and with the people of God are not crowded out. However, there is a spiritual or theological reason why exemplary, hortatory presentations that urge us to do better by following these saintly examples can be counterproductive.

When grace is overlooked, legalism abounds

The simplest way of stating the danger of the exemplary approach is that it focuses on people and their deeds, and not on what God says and does. It is not a matter of one or the other, but of allowing God's word to establish the principles that lie behind what we should be doing. Both the acts of God and the responses of people should be put into perspective. Other people's examples may or may not illustrate these principles. One of the most sinned-against biblical principles is that of the grace of God in the gospel as the pattern, motive and power for Christian living. Let us take the example of Jesus. The Christian church has always acknowledged the role of the imitation of Christ as a valid principle in Christian living. After all, if we cannot see Jesus as an example of the godly life, who can we see in this role? Yet the church has recognized, when it has sought to understand things in the light of the Bible, that Jesus did not come *primarily* to set an example. Following Jesus was not, for the disciples, solely a matter of trying to be like him in his perfect humanity. It was first of all a matter of believing in him as the unique fulfiller of the Old Testament prophecies of the Christ, the Saviour who was to come to do for them what they were powerless to do for themselves. To keep the biblical perspective we need to see that imitation of Jesus is secondary to and the derivative of the acceptance of his unique role in doing things that can never be merely imitated. The Christian disciple imitates elements of Jesus' life and ministry such as serving one another and even laying down one's life for others. But such serving can never achieve what Jesus' serving achieved in the forgiveness of sins and the salvation of all who believe.

At root, the task of Christian living stems from the grace of God's actions for us in Christ. The tragedy of the church in the medieval period was that this relationship between God's grace and our works was radically altered through a redefinition of grace.[1] How people

---

1. The medieval church shifted the idea of grace from the main focus that it has in the Bible. Instead of grace being the undeserved mercy of God that is primarily expressed in the historic acts of God in Christ, it became more the sanctifying act of God in the believer. Grace in baptism and through the

lived the Christian life was seen as the grounds of their acceptance with God. In theological language, sanctification (personal holiness) became the grounds for justification (right standing with God); how holy we are was regarded as the basis of our acceptance by God. The sixteenth-century Reformers saw the problem in this and proceeded to put the gospel right side up by stressing the centrality of the substitutionary work of Christ for us. The work that Christ did *for* us is primary, and it is the only basis or grounds for the work that Christ does *in* us by his Spirit. The work of Christ's Spirit within us is to enable us to do what we strive to do in conforming our lives to godliness.

Since prayer is an aspect of our santification, our development or growth in godliness, it too must be understood as the fruit of what Christ has done for us. This is often the missing dimension in books and sermons on prayer. In this book I will explore the way that our prayer relates to the God who has acted for us in the life, death and resurrection of Jesus. Problems emerge when the task of praying is urged without the motive and pattern of the unique saving role of Jesus. It then becomes a legalistic burden that cannot promote godliness. I will not be concerned primarily with the practical details of how we should discipline ourselves to give enough time for prayer. While practical matters are important, my main purpose is to address foundational questions of what happens in prayer, how it is possible, where it should be directed, and what we should expect of it.

If my assessment has been accurate, it follows that many of our problems with prayer stem from a failure to understand the relationship of our praying to the ministry of Jesus, including his praying. A wrong perspective on prayer may well come from thinking of it as playing a part in establishing our acceptance with God. Prayer that is not the grateful response of the justified sinner is likely to degenerate into an attempt to gain acceptance. Then again, if the sole motive to

---

sacraments of the church was infused into the soul so that the resulting holiness of life might bring about justification or acceptance with God. The Reformers, including Luther and Calvin, led the way in returning grace to the objective attitude of God towards the undeserving (ungodly) sinner on the basis of Christ's work for us.

pray is, as I have heard it put in sermons, 'Jesus got up early to pray, so how much more do we need to get up early to pray', it is missing the grace of God in the gospel. 'He did it, therefore we ought to' is not the perspective of the gospel unless it linked with, 'He did it for us because we are unable to do it as we ought.'

It comes down to the avoidance of legalism. Legalism is the name we give to the attempt to achieve righteousness, a right standing with God, by our own efforts in fulfilling the requirements of God. At root we understand that legalism is wrong, but we easily succumb to it without appreciating what is going on. The only answer to this is to keep reminding ourselves of what God has done for us as the central focus of the Bible. It is true that the Bible contains many commands and exhortations to Christian behaviour. That is not in doubt. However, when a biblical text dealing with the things we ought to do is appropriated apart from its wider context of the good news that God has first acted for us, legalism will begin to manifest itself. Elsewhere I have referred to the danger of losing sight of this principle when preaching a series of sermons on the New Testament epistles.[2] If, for example, we find that sermon number four on, say, Ephesians moves on to the ethical implications of the gospel, the preacher would do well to make it clear that there exists in the epistle the all-important connection with the gospel that earlier sermons in the series would have dealt with. The same tendency to the fragmenting of the overall message of a passage may affect our daily Bible reading. This occurs when there is a failure to recognize the connections between the different parts within a particular book. This easily happens when we are so concerned to ask questions about the application of the day's reading that we fail to relate that portion to the overall message. It can also occur at the wider level of reading a passage from the Old Testament and thinking about it without consciously relating it to the fulfilment of the Old Testament in Christ. Some Old Testament texts, such as those that deal with certain details of Israel's ceremonial law, cry out for us to make some adjustment for the fact that Jesus has come. Because

2. See G. Goldsworthy, *Preaching the Whole Bible as Christian Scripture* (Grand Rapids: Eerdmans, 2000), p. 118f.

Christians do not go in for the kind of rituals and sacrifice of animals prescribed in the Old Testament, we are forced to try to relate such things to the fulfilment they undergo in the ministry of Christ. But other faith matters in the Old Testament, such as the prayers in the Psalms, are quite easily read as they stand and we simply assume the connection with ourselves. Whether or not we reflect on this assumption and the grounds for it is another matter.

A place to start

We should at least raise the question of what we mean when we talk about prayer and praying. The answer seems so obvious that you might question the need to waste time in this way. However, the problems mentioned above are real and they indicate the need to be clear about the practice of prayer. Let us begin with a simple working definition that we can adjust, modify, qualify or alter in any way that our investigation of the biblical data leads us.

> Prayer is talking to God.

It would be hard to provide a simpler or more basic definition than that! It is simple, but is it sufficient? We might reflect on this definition and then be moved to ask questions such as:

- Is it really possible to talk to God?
- Does he want to listen to us?
- What kinds of things can or should we say to him?
- Will it make any difference if we pray or not?

Is it good enough, for example, simply to point to the universal phenomenon of people of all religions making some kind of address to their deities? If prayer is talking to God, what do we call talking to other gods? Is twirling a prayer wheel prayer? Coming closer to home, does God hear the prayer of the unconverted person who may cry out in desperation and as a last resort? Perhaps we have had a less complicated introduction to prayer by growing up within a Christian home where prayer was a regular thing. Perhaps we got converted, started going to church, and found praying was simply part of what was done when Christians came together. For some it may be sufficient simply to note that throughout the Bible we find the people of God at prayer.

It should be noted that the word pray has a rather specific original meaning in English. It means to ask someone for something. This reflects the fact that the biblical words for prayer are primarily words for asking or entreating God. However, in common usage among Christians the word prayer has come to be applied to a variety of types of address to God, and we must enquire into the legitimacy of this extension of meaning.

I want to try to get behind the practices of the people observed in the pages of the Bible and ask what else the Bible tells us about prayer. The logic of addressing God in prayer may seem to be quite easily put thus:

> Persons talk to one another.
> God is a person and so is each one of us.
> Therefore God talks to us, and we talk to him.

There is indeed a vital principle tied up in this simple equation that I want to explore. But a word of caution is in order. We are prone to begin thinking about God as if he is an infinitely good and infinitely powerful version of ourselves. This is fraught with danger, and the syllogism above will need some adjustment if we are to avoid that danger. I was once given the following wise advice: 'If you want to keep your thinking on track, always begin with God and work down to us. Do not start with us and try to work back to God.' Obviously we cannot divorce ourselves as thinking, self-conscious human beings from the equation. But questions about who God is, what he is like, and how he has acted to save us should be considered prior to questions about who we are and how we should live and pray. The latter questions will be totally out of focus if we do not seek to answer them in the light of the former.

The aim of this book

In the course of this book I shall address some of these matters by looking at the biblical principles that lie behind all the texts that we might call upon to support the idea that Christians should pray. I want to get a handle on prayer by asking why it is there in the first place; what its role is in our fellowship with God; and what is involved in praying as a Christian. I want to try to get beyond a mere description of prayers in the Bible to the underlying principles at work. More than anything I want to avoid leaving my readers with a sense of guilt because they feel that their prayer life is not what it should be. There are, of course, some attitudes that we should feel guilty about if we persist in them. While we are still tied to our sinful natures, constant repentance of our unwillingness to engage with God is necessary. However, I suspect that many Christians simply need the right kind of encouragement that comes from a biblical perspective on the matter.

Those readers who are familiar with some of my other writing will know that I advocate the investigation of any biblical theme or concern by using the method of biblical theology. Do not be put off by this technical term; it is a shorthand way of referring to the investigation of the biblical evidence on a given topic as it unfolds throughout the whole process of God's dealings with his people recorded in the Bible. This does not require us to examine every book of the Bible exhaustively, but it does require that we try to locate the key places that relate to the topic under examination, and seek to understand the individual texts as they relate to the process of the one big story of the Bible. Such a biblical-theological investigation can be pursued at a technical level, or can be undertaken in a simple, non-technical way. I want to attempt the latter without being simplistic or overlooking vital evidence. Even at the non-technical level, this will involve us in some thought-provoking concepts and theological ideas. It is, however, worth persevering for the sake of greater understanding.

In the next four chapters we will consider the four questions raised by my simple definition of prayer: prayer is talking to God. We will examine in turn these concerns:

- Is prayer possible? What is the reality of prayer?
- Does God listen? What is the basis of prayer?
- How do we know what to say? What is the source of prayer?
- Does praying make any difference? What is the enabling of prayer?

We will follow this with an examination of the ideas linked by Jesus in the 'Lord's Prayer.' We will then track the path of the practice of prayer as it unfolds in the history of Israel and through to the New Testament.

Knowing God and having fellowship with him

If prayer is talking to God, who is this God that we talk to? At the level of our human experience, we can assert the following: how we talk to people, and what we say, will to a large extent be governed by how well we know them. The better we know them, and the more we know about them, the more intimate our speaking will be. Talking to a complete stranger may involve a rather tentative approach in which a few formal pleasantries are offered, perhaps a request made (of a shop assistant or a receptionist), or some response given to what is said to us. If a stranger approaches us with a request for some money, we may perceive him or her as threatening, as benign and needy, as a fraud, or as out of touch with reality. Our reply and consequent behaviour will reflect our perception or knowledge of this person. We may be totally out of touch with the reality of the situation and respond inappropriately. At the risk of seeming to ignore my own warning about starting with ourselves, I want to say that there is a connection between how we speak to one another and how we speak to God. I have already drawn the analogy between our personal encounter with the living God and our encounters with people. Thus, we can say that how we know God will greatly affect the way we approach him in prayer. This can be shown from Scripture. As we proceed I will try to show something of the biblical teaching about knowing God and having fellowship with him, and what this implies for prayer. We also need to recognize that God has spoken to us first in his word, and this reflects how well he knows us and our need of his grace.

Summary

- There are a number of problems that Christians perceive in relation to prayer that often stem from a failure to understand the nature of prayer.
- The solutions to difficulties with prayer do not lie primarily in godly examples or in legalistic requirements but in understanding the principles involved in prayer.
- We need to understand how prayer relates to our knowledge of God and of his grace in the gospel.

Pause a moment . . .

When you think about your practice of prayer and, perhaps, some of the problems you experience, do you mainly consider:

- what you are like as a praying Christian, or
- what God is like as our heavenly Father who saves us?

2 Finding the reality of prayer

Who spoke first?

The biblical answer to the question 'Who spoke to God first?' might seem obvious. Surely it was Adam, or maybe an angel. Genesis 1 tells us that God created all things by his word, including human beings. So the more basic question is, 'Who spoke first of all?' According to this narrative, speech occurs in this order: first God speaks to, or within, himself the word of creation, 'Let there be light.' Similar words precede the creation on each day. On the sixth day he speaks the distinctive word by which the human race is brought into being. Then he addresses the humans with the words, 'Be fruitful and multiply and fill the earth and subdue it and have dominion over the fish of the sea and over the birds of the heavens and over every living thing that moves on the earth.' (Gen. 1:28). However, we find no reference to Adam replying to God until after the dreadful act of disobedience recorded in Genesis 3. There is something ominous about God's call, 'Where are you?' (v. 9) In shame the humans hide from God but he seeks them out. Adam's first recorded words are born out of his guilt and fear: 'I heard the sound of you in the garden, and I was afraid, because I was naked, and I hid myself.'(Gen. 3:10). If it is true that

Adam was the first to address God, then we have the added problem of the fact that he spoke out of shame. This might seem to be a poor basis for understanding prayer.

Since it is recorded that God spoke first, it is worth pondering why he spoke the creation into being by his word? Why did he not think it into being, or (metaphorically) snap his fingers? Why this emphasis on word? It is so pervasive throughout Scripture that we tend to take it for granted. In fact, it is so pervasive in human existence that we cannot imagine an existence without speech.[1] Being human is so utterly inseparable from being speakers to other humans that to be permanently speechless is inconceivable. We will need to look further at this word-centredness of the biblical message. God speaks the universe into being and then he speaks to those whom he has created in his image. Word dominates the notion of God creating and communicating with people.

This divine communication with people in the Old Testament is primarily through the words of the prophets. Reflecting on this, the epistle to the Hebrews begins by connecting the prophetic word with Christ: 'Long ago, at many times and in many ways, God spoke to our fathers by the prophets, but in these last days he has spoken to us by his Son' (Heb. 1:1–2). John also understands Jesus to be the focus of God's word: 'And the Word became flesh and dwelt among us.' (John 1:14). The end of the story, as Peter tells us, is to be a similar word-event: 'By the word of God heavens existed long ago and an earth was formed . . . by the same word the present heavens and earth have been reserved for fire, being kept until the day of judgment and destruction of the godless' (2 Pet. 3:5, 7, NRSV). It is clearly the nature of God that, just as he made all things by his word and will judge by his word, so also he communicates by his word. This word expresses itself most clearly in Jesus of Nazareth.

Note that the Genesis account of the creation of the humans on the sixth day is introduced by a unique word of God. Up to this point the creation events are introduced by phrases such as, 'Let there be . . .'

---

1. Here we must include sign language and other means of substituting, if necessary, for the passing of air over the vocal chords. Obviously, if God speaks, this does not presuppose that he has vocal chords.

But when it comes to the climax of creation, God says, 'Let us make man in our image, after our likeness' (Gen. 1:26). Bible commentators have argued for centuries about the significance of the use of the plural 'Let us'. Some would say that it shows that Moses understood in some way that God is Trinity.[2] It is difficult to say to what extent Moses would have been able to express the doctrine of the Trinity. I would prefer to say that what God has inspired the writer to record here is consistent with the Christian understanding of God as Trinity. It is consistent with the fact that when we get to the New Testament we find that the Word who became flesh is also described as the Creator of all things (John 1:3).

It is clear from the prologue to John's Gospel that John regarded Jesus as God the Creator. If we now add to the picture what is said right back in Genesis 1:2 that the Spirit of God was present and involved in the creation, we have a glimpse of the Trinity being involved in the creation by word. Does God speak to himself when he says 'Let us'? Surely the answer is yes. The Genesis account shows us that God has a deliberative word by which he creates. There is no-one else there but God, although some have suggested that God is addressing a kind of angelic council. This does not seem likely since nowhere are humans explicitly described as being made in the image and likeness of angels, nor is it said that angels assisted in creation.[3] If he is not speaking to angelic beings, then to whom is he speaking? Does it make sense for God to talk to himself when we regard such activity by humans as a little odd? It does make sense if we understand something of what it means for God to be Trinity. It is not the easiest idea to grasp, and in the end we are forced to confess that we can barely conceive of God being three persons yet one God. We

---

2. The assumption that Moses wrote the whole Pentateuch is traditionally held but dismissed by much modern criticism. It is not really at issue here. Given that Moses mediated the law, which constitutes the bulk of the Pentateuch, it is entirely appropriate to refer to the whole corpus as the work of Moses even if he did not write every word of it (for example, the account of his own death).
3. The statement is: 'Let us make man in our image, after our likeness', and it implies that humans are in the image of the speaker and of the one(s) addressed.

struggle to avoid the two opposite errors either of conceiving of God as three separate Gods, or of thinking of his three-ness as merely a convenient way of describing the different ways in which the one God acts.

Genesis 1:26–28 makes sense in the light of the further teaching of the Bible that we are able to speak to God in response to his word to us. Being created in the image of God we reflect certain characteristics of God, and speech would seem to be one of them. Thus, we see that the God who made us in his image is a speaking God within himself, and that the one who came to be for us the perfect image of God is shown to speak with God while here on earth. Jesus is not only the Word of God who has come in the flesh, but as the true image of God he speaks the truly human word to the Father in heaven. Putting together all the evidence that we have about Jesus Christ, we have to say that he is:

- the God who speaks
- the word of God that is spoken to us
- the perfectly obedient human listener to that word, and
- the one who speaks to God the perfect human response to the word of God.

We conclude that God speaks within himself before anything else exists and that, before ever human beings existed, the prior word spoken to God the Father is the word of God the Son. As the one who spoke to the Father before the creation, and as the God-Man who spoke to his Father in heaven, he becomes our focus for understanding the reality of prayer as a human address to God. As we examine these aspects of biblical revelation we are confronted with the uniqueness of the God of the Bible. We will see as we proceed that the Christian understanding of prayer goes hand in hand with the self-revelation of God and, thus, with our knowledge of him.

The perfect image of God

Certain facts about Jesus and prayer are clear. First, Jesus taught his disciples that they should pray. In the Sermon on the Mount (Matt.

5 – 7) Jesus teaches not only the Lord's Prayer as the pattern for prayer, but he also teaches the disciples about such things as where and when to pray, who to pray for, and what kind of praying to avoid. In his ministry he tells them parables about prayer to encourage them. In other places we find his exhortations to pray in certain circumstances such as the coming tribulation. He assures them of the efficacy of believing prayer, and warns them of the need for the right disposition for prayer (Matt. 9:38; 24:20; 26:41; Mk. 13:18, 33; 14:38).

The second thing that we note about Jesus and prayer is his own practice of it. He prayed alone in lonely places, and he prayed with others in the synagogue and in the temple. Some of the unique events in his life and ministry are linked with his prayer. Prayer is the context in which he puts the question that leads to Peter's confession that Jesus is the Christ (Luke 9:20). Prayer is the occasion of the transfiguration of Christ (Luke 9:28–36), an event that concludes with the three disciples hearing the testimony of God to his Son, to whom they should listen (v. 35). In the Garden of Gethsemane Jesus agonizes in prayer prior to his arrest (Matt. 26:36–44). Three times, while on the cross, he is recorded as crying out to his Father in heaven (Matt. 27:46; Luke 23:34, 46).

The speaking to God that is so much a part of Jesus' life is one aspect of his being the perfect image of God. If prayer is thus linked with being made in God's image, is it a uniquely human activity? There is another way in which the Bible describes part of the creation addressing God. While it is true that only human beings are created in God's image, yet the Scriptures put forward the idea of all creation addressing God in praise. This is seen as a kind of accompaniment to the songs of praises of the redeemed people of God:

> Let the sea roar, and all that fills it;
>   the world and those who dwell in it!
> Let the rivers clap their hands;
>   let the hills sing for joy together
> before the Lord, for he comes to judge the earth.
>
> (Ps. 98:7–9)

While nature does not speak as we do, this is more than mere poetic imagery. It expresses the involvement of the whole of the created order in the redemption of God's people. The sin of mankind brought the whole of creation under judgment, and the redemption of mankind will be accompanied by the renewal of the whole creation. Paul expresses the relationship between creation's praise and our redemption thus:

> For the creation waits with eager longing for the revealing of the sons of God. For the creation was subjected to futility, not willingly, but because of him who subjected it, in hope that the creation itself will be set free from its bondage to decay and obtain the freedom of the glory of the children of God.
>
> (Rom. 8:19–21)

There is, however, a clear distinction between human speech and the involvement of the creation as a whole in the redemptive grace of God. The metaphor of the rejoicing or expectant creation expresses an important point of unity, but the distinction between humans and the rest of creation is essential to maintain. The prayer or praise of creation is a metaphor expressing this sharing in judgment and redemption with the human race.

This metaphor of speech is also applied to the testimony of the created order to the glory of God. Yet it is a wordless speech; words without words; the very existence of the creation being eloquent of the one who created all things:

> The heavens declare the glory of God,
> and the sky above proclaims his handiwork.
> Day to day pours out speech,
> and night to night reveals knowledge.
> There is no speech, nor are there words,
> whose voice is not heard.
> Their measuring line goes out through all the earth,
> and their words to the end of the world.
>
> (Ps. 19:1–4)

But when we come to consider human speech it is quite different from the way creation 'speaks'. Human speech is not a metaphor, but is rather the source of the metaphor that is applied to the rest of the creation. Thus, it is an important characteristic that distinguishes us from the rest of creation.

In considering the biblical testimony to Jesus as the praying Word of God, as the incarnate God who calls upon the Father in prayer, we cannot conclude that such a word-address to God has its origin in humans. It begins to look as though the Bible is teaching us that God spoke uniquely to the first humans because they were made in his image. He is a discoursing God within the context of the history of redemption for the very reason that he is also a discoursing God within himself from all eternity. When the Bible refers to God speaking, whether to people or to himself, this is not a way of speaking about God that attributes to him human qualities. The Bible does contain such anthropomorphisms (speaking of God as if he possessed human form) when it speaks about God as having eyes or a mighty arm, and so on. But we must be careful not to turn all the analogies between God and humans into a 'humanizing' of God.

Prayer and the knowledge of God as Trinity

Let me now suggest some important ways in which we can follow the principle of beginning our reasoning with the knowledge of God. We do not talk about the personhood of God, or describe the Trinity as three 'persons', as a mere anthropomorphism forced on us by the need to conceive of a personal being greater than us. Nor do we use trinitarian language simply to highlight the different roles of God (Creator = Father; Redeemer = Son; Indweller = Spirit). Above all, the personal nature of God is not a mere analogy with our personal nature. Rather, Christian theology has always acknowledged that the only satisfactory explanation for our human personhood is that it has its source in a personal Creator. If we extend that to the qualities that are distinct to human personhood, we also have to confess that our ability to think, reason and express ourselves creatively stems from our creation in the image of the thinking, reasoning, creative God. The ability we have to speak to each other in human discourse, which reflects thinking, reasoning and creativity, is derived from God in whose image we are made. Some theologians who argue the case for Christianity against non-Christian beliefs have used this point to good effect. When non-Christians use logic, reason and speech to try to refute Christianity, they are in fact demonstrating its truth by their very use of logic, reason and speech, yet they cannot see it. The reason they cannot see it is, as Paul puts it in Romans 1:18–23, that '. . . by their unrighteousness [they] suppress the truth . . . and their foolish hearts were darkened'.

Our most important characteristic as human beings is the one that God indicates. We are created in his image, and to know ourselves properly we must know God as he reveals himself. One problem with trying to establish the exact meaning of being created in God's image and after his likeness is that the constituents of these two terms are not listed in an unambiguous way in Scripture.[4] Up to this point I have argued, in effect, that we shall only get a proper grasp of the meaning of the image of God in us by observing the nature of the one who perfectly bore that image. Two things above all concern us in this regard: first, that Christ is the image of God who has come among us (2 Cor. 4:4; Col. 1:15; see also Heb. 1:3), and secondly, that although we at present bear a sinfully marred image of God, we shall be conformed to the image of Christ and thus the true image of God will be restored in us (Rom. 8:29; 1 Cor. 15:49; 2 Cor. 3:18; Col. 3:10).

Jesus the praying Word

We must return to the main subject of prayer. It has been necessary to examine the reality of prayer in terms of God himself and the way he has made us. Jesus, as noted above, taught his disciples many things about prayer so that they might understand what it is to pray. But he did more than teach them about prayer, for he himself prayed for them. The clearest example of this is in the so-called high-priestly prayer of Jesus recorded in John 17. This comes as the climactic sequel to Jesus' final discourse with the disciples before his death (John 13:31 – 16:33). John presents this prayer as virtually a continuation of the

4. Philip Hughes, *The True Image* (Grand Rapids: Eerdmans, 1989), chapter 5, argues that the image, which marks humans apart from the animals, consists of personality, spirituality, rationality, morality, authority and creativity.

words to the disciples, except now Jesus addresses his Father in heaven.

Vern S. Poythress has argued strongly that the high-priestly prayer shows us that the incarnate Son of God speaks to the Father in a way that involves both his being as a human and his being as the eternal second person of the Trinity.[5] He speaks as the God-Man, and he thus speaks out of both his humanity and his deity. Poythress argues, and I think he is right in this, that this particular prayer points to the relationship betweem God the Son and God the Father from all eternity. Integral to this relationship is discourse. The fact that the Son of God[6] is at the same time God the Son incarnate shows that discourse in prayer reflects or images the divine discourse that characterizes the relationships within the Trinity. In distinguishing the titles 'God the Son' and 'Son of God' it is important to note the following:

- The deity of Christ is not in doubt when we stress the use of the term 'Son of God' in many biblical passages as referring to the true and sinless humanity of Jesus.
- The proof that Jesus is God the Son, the second person of the eternal Trinity, does not depend on passages referring to him as the Son of God.
- It may be argued that some passages referring to Jesus as the Son of God refer to his deity, or that they embrace the fact that he is the God-Man (both God and man).
- The distinction is important because of the danger of losing sight of the humanity of Jesus in the process of arguing (against the gainsayers) for his divinity. The two natures of Christ are equally important for our salvation.[7]

---

5. Vern S. Poythress, *God-Centered Biblical Interpretation* (Phillipsburg: Presbyterian and Reformed Publishing, 1999), pp. 16–25.
6. The title 'Son of God' is applied here in the manner used by Luke in his account of Jesus' baptism (Luke 3). The use of the genealogy indicates that the title refers to his humanness, his descent from Adam, and his being representative of Israel, the son of God (see Exod. 4:22–23; Hos. 11:1).
7. See 1 John 4:1–3, where the denial of Jesus' humanity is called the spirit of the antichrist.

One can understand why some theologians have proposed a kind of covenant or pact between the Father and the Son, in effect an agreement that the Son should take upon himself human nature and be the Saviour of God's people. This is sometimes referred to as the covenant of redemption.[8] The grounds for this idea of a covenant comes from recognizing that redemption is conveyed to its objects in a covenantal form, and that this redemptive work of God stems from a discourse and pact within the Trinity.

Thus in John 17, as Jesus prays, he refers to the authority that the Father has given him (v. 2). He speaks of the Father as having sent him (v. 3) and as having given him work to do (v. 4). He refers to the glory he had beforehand with the Father in his presence, a glory he asks to be restored (v. 5). He speaks of his people as given him by the Father, and as having the words given to the Son by the Father (vv. 6–8). Since the disciples of Christ are the Father's gift to the Son, Jesus prays that they will be protected from the evil one while they remain in the world. This divine discourse is not confined to the Father and the Son, for Jesus has already promised that the Spirit of God will come to his disciples and guide them into the truth. While Jesus claims that he himself is the truth (John 14:6), this truth comes from the Father (John 14:10). The Spirit testifies to Jesus by speaking 'whatever he hears' (John 16:13). Thus, the Father is described as the source and the sender of the truth into the world. The Spirit also hears the truth and will convey it to the people of God. This truth is reflected in the prayer of Jesus, who is the true image of God. In prayer he expresses both his deity as God the Son, and his humanity as the Son of God. The reality of prayer is thus established in the true image of the speaking God.

One further point should be made. The earthly intercession of Jesus is inseparable from his wider saving work. The teaching that Jesus gave about prayer should always be seen as one aspect of being caught up in the saving work of God. The act of praying, and the content of the prayer, is part of being saved. This salvation includes

---

8. See, for example, the discussion of this subject in Thomas McComiskey, *The Covenants of Promise: A Theology of the Old Testament Covenants* (Grand Rapids: Baker Book House, 1985), chapter 4.

the whole range of God's redemptive work in making us his people, in giving us the grace of perseverance, and in bringing us to the final consummation in glory. In short, we can say that the whole notion of prayer, and particularly its content, is tied to what the gospel is and how its goals are achieved. This includes such things as praying for our daily bread, since our bodily sustenance is a work of grace that anticipates the resurrection of the body. This relationship of prayer to the gospel cannot be stressed too much, for it provides the basis for any answer we give to the question of what can we legitimately pray for.

Jesus the ascended intercessor

Another aspect to the biblical perspective on Jesus and the reality of prayer needs to be considered. The ascension of Jesus is critical to our understanding of our present existence as the people of God. When the disciples were faced with the fact of Jesus' death it was a rude shock to them because they had not anticipated it. They should have known better, as Jesus indicated to the two travellers to Emmaus (Luke 24:18–27, particularly v. 25). Yet, once the demoralized disciples recognized the resurrected Jesus, their hope revived and they began to look forward to the restoration of the kingdom of God (Acts 1:6). But, their question, 'Lord, will you at this time restore the kingdom to Israel?', was somewhat wide of the mark. Their notion of an earthly restoration of the temple and Jerusalem was still in need of some transformation in the light of who and what Jesus was. The ascension and the subsequent coming of the Holy Spirit at Pentecost provided this transformation. Jesus' answer to their enquiry about the restoration, and the effect of the Spirit's coming, demonstrates that the kingdom comes through the preaching of the Spirit-empowered gospel in all the world (Acts 1:7–8). The ascension means that, at a time known only to the Father, Jesus will return in a manner similar to his going, and the consummation of the kingdom will be manifested in the whole universe (Acts 1:11).

But what is Jesus doing between his ascension and his return in glory? We can answer the question biblically according to two perspectives. The first concerns Jesus' relationship to his people on earth, and the second concerns Jesus' relationship to his Father in heaven. In looking at the first perspective we see that Jesus, as he had promised his disciples, is earth-directed; he maintains his concern and involvement in the coming of the kingdom here and now in this period between his ascension and his coming again. He does not leave his people as orphans when he withdraws from them, but sends the Spirit and, in view of the Trinity being one, he is himself thus present with us here (John 14:18–20; 22–23; 15:4–5). It is important that we understand that Jesus, in terms of his bodily resurrection, is not here, he is in heaven. But it is also true to say that he is here; he makes himself present to us by his Spirit, and it is by his Spirit that he dwells with or in us. This is the Spirit of God who is also the Spirit of Christ (Rom. 8:9–11). It is important that we maintain this distinction between Christ's absence and his presence. The absent Christ performs an important function for us in heaven.

This trinitarian perspective pervades not only the discourse of John 14 – 16, but is at the heart of Paul's treatment of the Spirit-filled life in Romans 8. Note the progression of Paul's argument in this passage:

- The Christian life is a life lived in relation to the Spirit (vv. 1–13).
- When we cry out to the Father, the Spirit bears witness that we are children of God and joint heirs with Christ (vv. 14–17).
- This life in the Spirit involves us in suffering that is shared by the yet-to-be-redeemed creation (vv. 18–25).
- Our prayer to God is assisted by the intercession of the Spirit (vv. 26–27).
- We have been predestined to be conformed to the image of the Son (vv. 28–30).
- We are more than conquerors because of what Christ has done for us, and because he now intercedes for us (vv. 31–39).

Thus, although Christians are bound to suffer in various ways, nothing can separate us from the love of God in Christ. Paul portrays our situation in terms of the absolute sovereignty of God in foreknowledge and predestination, and over the whole process of our salvation from start to finish.

Paul also describes this process of salvation in a trinitarian way.

Note the trinitarian logic in the way the passage develops. First, salvation is characterized as life in the Spirit, as outlined above, and this Spirit is the one who intercedes for the saints according to the will of God (Rom. 8:26–27). Secondly, it is described as the sovereign work of the Father who foreknows his own, predestines, calls, justifies and glorifies them (Rom. 8:28–30). Thirdly, it is described as being based on the finished work of Christ, who died, was raised, and who now, being at the right hand of God, intercedes for us (Rom. 8:31–34). On this trinitarian basis Paul has confidence that the work of God is unshakeable and that 'we are more than conquerors through him who loved us' (v. 37). From the perspective of God, this is a description of his sovereign work. From the perspective of believers, this is a description of our perseverance to the end. Underlying our perseverance is the work of the Son for us, and the work of the Spirit in us. We are not alone in our suffering and our struggle to remain faithful. We have the intercession of the Spirit, who aids us in our role as praying and persevering saints, and the intercession of Christ, who beholds the face of our heavenly Father.[9]

The second aspect of Jesus' ministry after the ascension is his relationship with the Father. Yet this also has important ramifications for his people on earth as he intercedes for us. What is the significance of Jesus' intercessory prayer for us? In Romans 8:34, Paul includes it, without further discussion, as part of the saving work of Christ. The ascension was not simply the means of removing Jesus out of sight now that his work on earth is finished. The resurrection and ascension are the justification of Jesus in his humanity. By rising and ascending to heaven, the God-Man shows that his humanity is acceptable to God. Much of what Paul wrote stresses that what Jesus achieved in the flesh was on our behalf. Thus, in various places, Paul describes his own Christian existence, and ours, as bound up with the life, death, resurrection and ascension of Jesus. This union we have with Christ by faith means we can speak of ourselves as if we were there and actually participating in the events of Jesus' death and

---

9. The role of this intercessory prayer of Jesus in the perseverance of believers is discussed at greater length in G. C. Berkouwer, *Faith and Perseverance* (Grand Rapids: Eerdmans, 1958), chapter 5.

resurrection. The Christian is crucified with Christ (Gal. 2:19–20), buried with Christ in baptism (Rom. 6:4), made alive together with him, raised up with him and seated with him in heavenly places (Eph. 2:5–6). In other words, in God's eyes, it is the perfect humanity of Jesus, and his work that was done in the flesh, that count for our acceptance with God. In this, although Paul does not use the term, Jesus is our great high priest.

The Old Testament background to Jesus the intercessor

The most detailed treatment of Jesus fulfilling the office of priesthood is given in the epistle to the Hebrews. This epistle, along with the rest of the New Testament, constantly makes reference to the Old Testament background to the mission of Jesus. The priest in Israel was a man who stood as the representative of the people before God and as the representative of God before the people. He was a divinely appointed 'go-between'. The priest presented himself before God in the Holy Place, gaining access only through the blood of sacrifice. His principal role was to offer various sacrifices before the Lord and, by this means, to make atonement for the sins of the people. His other main function was to instruct the people in the law and in the ways of the Lord. The role of priest as intercessor is not explicit in the Old Testament and we are not told if any kind of liturgical prayer accompanied the sacrifices. The role of a sacrificing mediator certainly implies that a plea is presented before the Lord that the people be forgiven and accepted. We can only speculate that some kind of liturgy and prayer were integral to the service of the tabernacle and the temple.[10]

In the Old Testament it seems that intercession was regarded as more the function of the prophet than that of the priest. The prophets mediated God's word to the people and it is fitting that they too should mediate the people's word to God. Zedekiah, the king at the time when the Babylonians threatened the safety of Jerusalem, actually sends the priest Zephaniah to Jeremiah the prophet with the

10. There is plenty of evidence for liturgy and prayer in later Judaism.

request, 'Please pray for us to the LORD our God' (Jer. 37:3). God spoke to King Abimelech about Abraham, saying, 'He is a prophet, so that he will pray for you, and you shall live' (Gen. 20:7). But Psalm 99:6 makes the interesting observation that the priests interceded:

> Moses and Aaron were among his priests,
> Samuel also was among those who called on his name.
> They called to the LORD, and he answered them.

It becomes clear in verse 8 what sort of prayer is referred to here:

> O LORD our God, you answered them;
> you were a forgiving God to them,
> but an avenger of their wrongdoings.

We know of Moses' intercession for the rebellious Israelites at Sinai and in the desert (Exod. 34:9; Num. 11:2; 21:7; Deut. 9:26). Samuel prayed for the people as they continued to display their faithlessness (1 Sam. 7:5, 8; 12:19, 23). Both these men showed that, at times, the distinction between the roles of prophet and priest was blurred, as was the distinction between king and priest. It is clear that the role of the prophet is not, and can not be, independent of the role of the priest. In the New Testament the offices of prophet, priest and king are all applied to Jesus.

This background to the intercessory priesthood of the risen Christ helps us to understand its significance during this period between the ascension and the return of Christ. In heaven, Jesus remains the one mediator between God and humankind (1 Tim. 2:5–6). Hebrews stresses his priestly role, referring to Jesus' priesthood and Israel's priesthood on some forty occasions. The author is concerned to show both continuity and discontinuity between the old priesthood and the definitive priesthood of Christ, and demonstrates how the priesthood of Jesus does not suffer from the imperfection of Israel's priests, who needed to offer continual sacrifice for themselves as well as for the people. Christ's is an eternal and unblemished priesthood. He gathers up and fulfils all the functions of the mediator priest, and this includes presenting before the Lord his own perfect sacrifice made for our sins once for all.

What then does Jesus achieve by this perpetual intercession in heaven? It is obvious from the wider context of the Bible that he is not pleading a cause before an unwilling God. Rather, he came into our world to do the will of the Father and has not failed in the doing of it. It is the Father's gracious plan that he has fulfilled and, in so doing, he has glorified the Father. His intercession, then, is his identification and involvement with the will of the Father. If we started with Jesus as the ultimate word of God to humankind, the Word incarnate, we now see him in his exaltation as the ultimate word of humankind to God. His resurrection has shown that he is the perfectly acceptable advocate for us sinners. His very presence with the Father pleads our cause, but pleads it from the God who loves to give his true children what they ask. Since this role of Jesus is from start to finish on our account, it gives us confidence to 'draw near with a true heart in full assurance of faith' (Heb. 10:22). The intercession of Christ is the perpetual guarantee that we do not speak to thin air or to the ceiling when we pray through him. We have access to the Father through him who is the true image of God. Both Paul and the author of Hebrews assure us that there can be no ceiling to stop our prayers since we are accounted as being with Christ in the very presence of the Father.

God's speech and our knowledge of him

If we look back over our discussion thus far we see that the eternally speaking God has done an amazing thing in speaking. The thing to note is that he has *done* something. Speech is not simply words; it is intended to do things. The actual words recorded in Genesis 1 and 2 may not tell us all that God said to Adam and Eve, but the narratives indicate that God is doing a number of things by his word. All of these are relevant to our knowledge of God. In revealing himself by his word he is doing far more than expressing propositions or facts about himself, the world and mankind. Out of love, he created the universe, all that is in it, and human beings in his own image. He then speaks to the humans and gives them the framework for understanding God, the world and themselves. He has revealed the norms for the true knowing of anything, he has expressed his authority by setting limits and designating the nature and bounds of human freedom, and he has shown himself to be a God who is present with this people.[11]

It, of course, goes much further than creation; the whole of God's word as it testifies to the Word of God incarnate is God doing his work, which can be summed up as the process from creation to new creation. In all this work God does not merely reveal truths. Our knowledge of him is derived from what he says about what he does in creation and redemption. It is thus inseparable from the knowledge we have of ourselves as created and redeemed by God.[12] In the incarnation of Jesus, who is God's final word of revelation, God shows his sovereignty over all things, he reveals the way we are to understand the world and ourselves, and he comes among us to make his dwelling with people. To know God is to know this creating, sovereign, guiding God who is with us.

In the last chapter I suggested a definition of prayer thus:

> Prayer is talking to God.

In the light of the matters raised in this chapter we need, perhaps, to try to refine this definition. I propose the following:

> Prayer is our response to God as he speaks to us.

I also proposed in the last chapter that we could express the logic of addressing God thus:

---

11. See John M. Frame, *The Doctrine of the Knowledge of God* (Phillipsburg: Presbyterian and Reformed, 1987). Frame gives a helpful analysis of this by speaking of God's control, authority and presence.

12. The Reformer John Calvin gave expression to this interrelationship in the opening chapter of his great compendium of Christian doctrine, the *Institutes of the Christian Religion*. Calvin shows how our knowledge of God and our knowledge of ourselves are bound up with one another. If we reflect on the fact that we are primarily defined as created in God's image, and that God is revealed as the creator of all things, we can grasp something of this important point that Calvin makes.

Persons talk to one another.
God is a person and so is each one of us.
Therefore God talks to us, and we talk to him.

Again, in the light of our discussion, I want to suggest a more biblical way that puts the priority of God's speech in place:

All speech originates with the Persons of the Trinity.
God has made us persons in his image.
Therefore God talks to us, and we talk to him.

Our knowledge of God as the Trinity, three Persons in one God, is the foundation for our understanding of ourselves as discoursing people and as praying people. The more we grasp what it is for God to be as he is, the more we will grasp what it is for us to be as we are. What God is and what we are will determine how the discourse between us is shaped. To the extent that our perceptions of either God or ourselves are distorted, so our perceptions of prayer will be similarly distorted.

Summary

- It is the nature of God from all eternity that speaking characterizes the communication within the Trinity.
- The speaking God created all things by his word and made humans in his image.
- The creating Word has come in the flesh and prayed for his people while on earth.
- Having done all that is necessary for us to be restored to God, the risen and ascended Word now prays in heaven for his people.
- The true image of God shows that for us to be in Christ is to be restored to the image of God and, in him, to become praying people.

Pause a moment . . .

Have you ever reflected on our ability to communicate by speech, to think rationally and to be creative as:

- aspects of our being created in God's image, and
- redeemed and made perfect by Christ, the true image of God?

Can we really explain our personhood, and our ability to interact personally using speech, without recourse to a God who is Trinity?

3 The basis of all prayer

Sons of the Father

In his excellent study of the theology of prayer, Wayne Spear refers disapprovingly to theologian Paul Tillich's stated difficulty with the orthodox Christian view of the Trinity because of the problems it creates for prayer.[1] Spear rightly recognizes that, contrary to Tillich's view, the doctrine of the Trinity is essential to the proper understanding of prayer in the Bible. The clearest indication of the Trinity is the incarnation of God the Son. Jesus refers to his Father while at the same time indicating his own deity. He also promises his own Holy Spirit, who also comes from the Father. In this chapter I will examine

---

1. Wayne R. Spear, *The Theology of Prayer: A Systematic Study of the Biblical Teaching on Prayer* (Grand Rapids: Baker, 1979), p. 24. Tillich quite rightly refers to the confusion we may experience in knowing which person of the Trinity to pray to. There is also the human propensity to resolve the matter by a practical tritheism (three different Gods). However, the existence of difficulties in conceiving of the Trinity is not to be resolved by eliminating the biblical teaching.

some of the implications for prayer of Jesus being God the Son who has come in the flesh.

Connected with the sonship of Jesus is the fact that the New Testament speaks of Christians as sons of God. I want to show that this is central to the question of the acceptability of our prayers. But it does raise some questions about the status of women and the use of the word son. We need to clarify this in the light of some related modern concerns, especially that of inclusive language in Bible translation. There are some significant differences of opinions as to its validity.[2] Women have had legitimate grievances of many kinds that have a long and not too attractive history. Christian men should welcome attempts to restore to women their rightful equality and dignity. But when the push for inclusive language goes to extremes it is in danger of obscuring important distinctions in Scripture. This is because male and female are not in every case interchangeable.[3] Genesis stresses that God created us as male *and* female. Sometimes inclusive language can obscure relationships that are vital for our understanding of the way the gospel functions in saving us. A case in point is the New Revised Standard Version (NRSV) translation of certain passages in Paul's letter to the Galatians. This is one of the key places in the New Testament expounding the justification of sinners through faith. In Galatians 3 the argument focuses on Abraham and the promises God made to him. Abraham was justified by faith in the promises of God (v. 6) and this is the principle that now operates under the gospel (vv. 7–9). Thus, Christian believers inherit the blessings promised to Abraham; they are the descendants of Abraham, to whom the promises were originally made.

But in order to make this move from Abraham to the Christian believer, Paul shows that the offspring of Abraham, to whom the promises of God were originally made, is in fact Christ. In this

2. This usually takes the form of extending, for example, a reference to brothers to include sisters, or the translation of 'sons' as 'children', when the context indicates that no distinction in gender is implied.

3. Some advocates of equality argue as if it means sameness in all respects. They then have to trivialise the obvious differences that are more than biological.

compact argument Paul points to the fact that the whole Old Testament finds its fulfilment in Christ. It is thus our union with Christ that makes us, in him, the offspring of Abraham and heirs of the covenant blessings. The argument is summarized in the following passages:

> Now the promises were made to Abraham and to his offspring. It does not say, 'And to offsprings,' referring to many, but referring to one, 'And to your offspring,' who is Christ.
>
> (Gal. 3:16)

Behind this statement lies the whole process of the line of descent from Abraham through Israel, through the kingly line of David, to Jesus. This is the significance of the family tree of Jesus that Matthew uses to commence his Gospel. Christ, by virtue of who he was and what he came to do, is recognized to be the only faithful and true descendant of Abraham. How, then, do we fit in? Paul gives the answer thus:

> For as many of you as were baptized into Christ have put on Christ.
>
> (Gal. 3:27)

To 'put on' Christ is a metaphor expressing an important truth. It does not mean that we cease to be ourselves or that we are from that point on passive bearers of the life of Jesus within or around us. Paul's way of speaking is to express our unity with Christ with regard to our acceptance with God. When God looks on us to consider our acceptability, it is as if he sees only his perfectly acceptable Son. Baptism signifies a faith-union with Christ so that what belongs to Christ, in this case the promises made to Abraham, belongs to those who believe. So the logic is:

> And if you are Christ's, then you are Abraham's offspring, heirs according to promise.
>
> (Gal. 3:29)

To return to my remarks about inclusive language we note how this part of Paul's argument reaches its climax in Galatians 4.

> But when the fullness of time had come, God sent his Son, born of a woman, born under the law, in order to redeem those who were under the law, so that we might receive adoption as children. And because you are children, God has sent the Spirit of his Son into our hearts, crying, 'Abba! Father!' So you are no longer a slave but a child, and if a child then also an heir, through God.
>
> (Gal. 4:4–7 NRSV)

In every place in this passage where the NRSV has 'children' or 'child' the Greek indicates 'sons' or 'son'. The English Standard Version (ESV) has returned to the literal translation of the Greek and does not obscure the point as the NRSV does. Does it matter? After all, we can hardly argue that Paul has regard here for only the males of the species, especially since in Galatians 3:28 we have his clear affirmation of the unity of both male and female in Christ:

> There is neither Jew nor Greek, there is neither slave nor free, there is neither male nor female, for you are all one in Christ Jesus.

Can it affect our understanding of the argument if we make the language inclusive? In the first place it may obscure the relationship that all believers have with God, the relationship expressed in the statement, 'Because you are sons, God has sent the Spirit of his Son into our hearts' (Gal. 4:6). The strength of Paul's argument rests in the logic that, if we belong to the Son, what belongs to him belongs to us. All believers are sons of the Father, not as a matter of our gender, but as a matter of our union with the Son. This goes for both men and women.

It is as well to remind ourselves that the title Son of God as applied to Jesus in the New Testament refers to his humanity and his descent from Adam through Abraham and David. Bear in mind that Israel was named as God's firstborn son in Moses' confrontation with the King of Egypt:

> Thus says the LORD, Israel is my firstborn son, and I say to you, 'Let my son go that he may serve me.' If you refuse to let him go, behold, I will kill your firstborn son.
>
> (Exod. 4:22–23)

The prophet Hosea later recalled this status of sonship:

> When Israel was a child, I loved him,
>   and out of Egypt I called my son.
>
> (Hos. 11:1)

God promised David's son, who as king would represent the whole nation, that he would have the status of God's son:

> I will be to him a father, and he shall be to me a son.
>
> (2 Sam. 7:14)

At his baptism Jesus identifies with Israel, but the word from heaven is:

> You are my beloved Son; with you I am well pleased.
>
> (Luke 3:22)

As if to make clear the meaning of this sonship, Luke immediately gives us his version of Jesus' family tree. He works backwards from Jesus, the son of Joseph, son of Heli, son of Matthat, and so on, right down the line until he comes to Enos, son of Seth, son of Adam, *son of God*. Jesus, then, is declared by God to be the acceptable Adamite (human) and the acceptable Israelite (covenant people of God). Then, when Jesus is tempted in the desert he fulfils the human role of Adam but remains faithful. It is noteworthy that this temptation of the perfect human begins with the challenge, 'If you are the Son of God . . .' (Matt. 4:3). Jesus overcomes the temptation and thus demonstrates that he is truly the well-pleasing Son of God.

The point of all this is that we need to be clear about our status before God. Through faith in Jesus as our Saviour we are given the same status that he has as the perfectly acceptable human before God. He is the Son of God, and we need to remember that our union with him by faith means that we share that status. Our sonship is not a gender issue; it is a status issue. Outside of Christ, men are no closer to being sons of God than are women. In Christ our gender does not affect our standing with God either way. We are all one in Christ because we all share what belongs to him in his standing as Son of

God, the acceptable human being before God. So, by all means use inclusive language when it is appropriate. But, at the same time, do not dismiss Paul's use of language as merely an old-fashioned putting down of women. Paul did not invent the names of God, nor the designation of Israel or Jesus as the Son. What God has revealed we should joyfully receive.

Prayer belongs to the children of the Father

It should be evident where this is leading us in the matter of prayer. In the previous chapter we looked at the relationship of God the Son to the Father and how the image of God in us provides the link with the God who communicates by his word. The reality of prayer hinges on that relationship of being created in the image of God. We focus now on the sonship of Christ as the basis of prayer. We have looked at something of Paul's discourse in Galatians. In this letter he tells us, in effect, that the sons of God call out to him as Father:

> And because you are sons, God has sent the Spirit of his Son into our hearts, crying, 'Abba! Father!'
>
> (Gal. 4:6)

We cannot call on God as Father except through the Spirit of Christ. We must know the reality of being sons of the Father through faith in Jesus. Clearly we have to dispense with the idea of God as a notion we can shape according to our own aspirations. We know this important aspect of God's being our Father by knowing ourselves as his sons. Paul also expresses this relationship of prayer to our sonship in another passage very similar to the one in Galatians, except that here he speaks of the link being our adoption as sons:

> For you did not receive the spirit of slavery to fall back into fear, but you have received the Spirit of adoption as sons,[4] by whom we cry, 'Abba! Father!'

---

4. Greek: *huiothesias* (*adoption as sons*).

> The Spirit himself bears witness with our spirit that we are children[5] of God, and if children, then heirs — heirs of God and fellow heirs with Christ, provided we suffer with him in order that we may also be glorified with him.
> (Rom. 8:15–17)

This is an appropriate image because adoption implies that we are not natural-born children of the one who adopts us. Yet, legally, adoption bestows on the adopted person all the rights, privileges and heirship that would belong to a natural-born child. Hence our adoption bestows on us joint heirship with Christ.

If, as argued in the previous chapter, the reality of prayer is dependent on our being created in the image of God, does this not mean that all human beings have equal access to God in prayer? Clearly this is not the case. The reason lies in the rebellion of the human race against the Creator. The Bible does not give explicit statements on the impact of sin on the image of God in us. We are told that death resulted from sin, but our understanding of to what extent the image of God is affected by our sinful rejection of God is dependent on two things at least. The first is the biblical evidence for what human nature is like after the fall. The second is the evidence of the true image in Christ and what he had to do to enable the true image to be restored in us.

After the sin of Adam and Eve, the narrative of Genesis shows the progressive degradation of the human race, while at the same time maintaining that sinful human beings are still made in the image of God (Gen. 9:6). The downside is that human sinfulness is an all-pervasive condition that places us under sentence of death and eternal judgment.[6] The upside is that it is an expression of God's grace that he does not allow the race to descend completely to the depths that it lusts after by its rejection of the rule of God.

---

5. Here the Greek has *tekna* (*children*), which is appropriate since Paul's argument here is not explicitly relating our status to the sonship of Jesus.
6. Reformed theologians have stressed the effect of sin in terms of total depravity or total inability. This was never intended to imply that humans are as bad as they can possibly be. Rather it signifies that sin has corrupted the whole of us so that no motive, thought or action is free from this corruption.

Theologians have thus, on the one hand, sought to express the gravity of our fallen condition and, on the other hand, maintained the continuing dignity of mankind. John Calvin spoke of the sense of deity that all possess and which is expressed in the universal propensity for religion and a sense of right and wrong.[7]

Once we turn to the person of Christ and the work he came to do, there can be no doubt as to the gravity of the marring of the divine image in us. If we could reduce the status of Jesus to that of good teacher of a new and enlightened ethical way, or if we could see him as merely an example of sacrificial love, then we would have grounds for an optimistic assessment of our natural human condition. But if God had to become one of us to provide a new Man who performed on our behalf all the will of God for humans, and who died to pay the penalty for our rebellion, then the diagnosis is indeed serious. Doctors do not perform a heart-lung transplant to treat the common cold, nor do they amputate a leg above the knee to treat an ingrowing toenail! The gospel, rightly understood, reveals to us the destructive nature of our rebellion against God.

The measure of the image of God remaining in us sinners, then, is not the basis upon which we can establish confidence that we can respond to God in prayer and be listened to. The remnant of the image of God in all people explains our rationality and ability to think and speak. It also explains our sense of deity and convictions about right and wrong. But the rebellious sinner who prays does not do so in faithful submission to the one true God, but out of a defiant heart. Whatever the vestige of the image in us, the status of sonship was entirely repudiated in the rebellion of our first parents. However you understand our involvement in the original sin, the entire history of the human race would oppose the optimistic assessment that evil is merely a learning of bad habits from those who have gone before us. The doctrine of original sin rightly asserts that Adam sinned as

---

7. John Calvin, *Institutes of the Christian Religion*, Book I, chapter 3. Again we note that Reformed theologians have understood this in the context of common grace. This means that God does not allow humanity to be as bad as it wants to be. He preserves the race in a world that is fallen but still filled with the goodness of God.

our representative head, and therefore we all without exception share his guilt as well as his corrupted nature. Anyone who thinks this is unjust should also reflect on how willingly and unerringly they themselves have participated in this rebellion against God. If anyone really thinks they could avoid being a fallen son of Adam, they should just give it a go!

Now we need to revisit the evidence of Scripture relating to the fact that prayer belongs to the sons of God. This is clear from the Lord's Prayer (Luke 11:1–2) and the fact that this is the address of God's children to the Father (Rom. 8:15–17; Gal. 4:6). For prayer to be real this relationship must be real. Sonship of the Father belonged to all human beings until Adam and Eve repudiated it. As human beings our natural state is that we are now not children of God but, as Paul says:

> [The sons of disobedience] among whom we all once lived in the passions of our flesh, carrying out the desires of the body and the mind, and were by nature children of wrath, like the rest of mankind.
>
> (Eph. 2:3)

The human race no longer recognizes or possesses sonship of God; rather we are children of his righteous wrath against our rebellion. Furthermore, it is a mistake to suppose that the practice of religion is a good and noble thing. We must reject the modern notion that all religions, including Christianity, are essentially the same and lead us to the same God.[8] Religion is not evidence of people seeking God, but rather of people seeking to avoid the truth of the One God whose creation speaks eloquently of him. Religion is a counterfeit for the truth of God that he has revealed.[9] Paul, in Romans 1:21–25, tells us of this rejection of the evidence of God in creation

8. Interfaith dialogue is good if it helps people of different faiths live together with understanding, and without hatred and prejudice. But if it seeks to bring about some kind of religious amalgam it will inevitably fail.

9. Such noble thoughts and deeds carried out in the name of religion without Christ must therefore be judged as part of the seductive counterfeit of the truth.

and the substitution of false worship. We can conclude that, with the loss of our sonship, the privilege of addressing God as Father was also lost.

Jesus is the only son of the Father

The foregoing discussion can be summarized as follows:

- Prayer belongs to the sons of the Father.
- Sonship was lost to the human race when Adam sinned and lost his sonship.
- Israel was called to fulfil the role of son of God but failed all along the line.
- Finally a true Son of God, who was descended from Abraham through David, fulfilled all righteousness on our behalf.
- By faith in this true Son of God, we are united to him and share his sonship and become joint heirs with him of the promises of God.

In what sense, then, is God the Father of all people? God is universal Creator and Lord. He rules over the kings of the earth even though they deny it and are ignorant of it. But he does not call himself the universal Father. The fatherhood of God to Israel was born of grace and saving love. The fatherhood of God to the anointed king could only make sense in the context of God's redemptive purposes (see Ps. 89:26–29). All these sons of God in the Old Testament, including David and Solomon, failed miserably to live up to the responsibilities of sons of God. Along with this failure there is the anticipation that God will do a work that will make for himself a true and faithful people who serve him as he desires. The prophets anticipate a righteous shepherd king, a suffering servant, a people cleansed with water and Spirit, but no such righteous person appears in Israel. Not until Jesus is baptized can we almost hear the sigh of relief as God declares that (at last!) here is a Son with whom he is well pleased.

The answer to the dilemma of our lost sonship is that God provided a true son who came on our behalf. This is the heart of the gospel: Jesus Christ was the Son of God who lived the human life of sonship that we fail to live. All have sinned and go on falling short of the glory of God (Rom. 3:23).[10] We therefore need someone to achieve that glory for us by a life of unfailing righteousness before God. This is the neglected truth of the saving life of Christ (Rom. 5:10). The advocate that we sinners have in heaven is the righteous one (1 John 2:1–2). The saving life of Christ explains what it means for us to be clothed in his righteousness (Rom. 3:21–24; 1 Cor. 1:30; 2 Cor. 5:21; Gal. 3:26–29; Phil. 3:8–10; Col. 3:3–4; Rev. 7:14–15). He also died to pay the penalty for the lives of rebellion against the Father that we have lived (Mark 10:45; Gal. 3:13; 1 Pet. 2:24). Jesus is not only our righteous representative, but he is also our substitute who is accounted as sin on our behalf and pays the penalty for our rebellion against God. The sacrificial death of Christ and his saving life are complementary truths.

Jesus is the true son who calls on the Father on our behalf

When Jesus came to the grave of Lazarus some four days after his friend's death, he prayed with a confidence that we may sometimes lack:

> So they took away the stone. And Jesus lifted up his eyes and said, '*Father, I thank you that you have heard me. I knew that you always hear me,* but I said this on account of the people standing around, that they may believe that you sent me.'
>
> (John 11:41–42, italics mine)

The picture that we have been able to build up is this. The Father is well pleased with Jesus' sonship (Luke 3:22), and consequently he always hears him (John 11:41–42; 17:1–26). On this our confidence is grounded, because the basis of all prayer is the sonship of Jesus. Now, and this is the important point, we actually share Jesus' sonship with him by faith. How? To summarize what we have argued thus far: God puts the believer *into* Christ, so that everything that belongs

---

10. While the Greek verb *sinned* is in the past tense, *fall short* is in the present. This would seem to indicate that we continually fall short of God's glory.

to Christ's perfect humanity belongs to us. We have his righteousness (Rom. 3:21–22); his is the life that is presented to God so that we are accepted (Col. 3:4); he is our righteousness before God (1 Cor. 1:30). Justification by faith means that God looks on us and regards us with the same acceptance with which he regards Jesus. Now, we have a man in heaven *for us*, who always lives to make intercession for us (Heb. 7:25).

In Christ we are God's children and our prayer is heard

Paul tells us that the Spirit of Jesus is the praying Spirit:

> And because you are sons, God has sent the Spirit of his Son into our hearts, crying, 'Abba! Father!' So you are no longer a slave, but a son, and if a son, then an heir through God.
>
> (Gal. 4:6–7)

This means that our prayer, through Jesus, enjoys the same acceptance as his prayer, because we are heirs with him. When we trust Jesus to be on our behalf everything God requires from us, we can pray with confidence. It is crucial that we understand what our justification in Christ means, particularly for our failures. Jesus justifies our humanness by being for us, on our account, the true human Son of God. The only reason he left his glory in heaven and took upon himself human flesh and the role of a servant, was to do for us what we could not do for ourselves. There is no aspect of our humanity that he has not dealt with. Whenever and however we fail, we have an advocate to take our place and plead our cause. He does this on the basis of his own righteousness, not on the basis of our fervour or piety. I do not want to labour this point, but it is worth noting that Jesus has justified our prayer. In other words, as with every other aspect of our humanness in which we fall short of the glory of God, he provides for us the basis of full acceptance. In Christ we cannot be condemned as inadequate or 'failed' pray-ers. I should not think, because I don't pray as I ought, that God is less inclined to listen to me than he is to listen to some great prayer warrior.

As with every other aspect of our lives, our aim should be to strive to become in ourselves more like what we are in Christ. What we are in Christ is perfect, and this perfection will never be achieved in ourselves until we are raised in the resurrection at his coming again. It is nevertheless the goal towards which we strive.

Prayer and the knowledge of God the Son

Since prayer involves speaking to the God who has spoken to us, we have to conclude that the basis of our prayer is the dialogue between the Father and the Son, through the Spirit. Without this intra-trinitarian speech there would be no human speech, to God or anyone else. We also conclude that the basis of our prayer is the sonship of Jesus to the Father and his perfect fulfilment of the role of the created sonship of human beings. This he has done *for* us in his life, death and resurrection. Justification by faith is at the heart of prayer in that the incarnate Word of God has fulfilled for us both the divine and the human aspects of our relationship with God. To pray 'Abba, Father' from the heart is to stand consciously in our justification and to express with confidence our union with Christ who motivates and patterns our prayer, and who justifies our inadequate prayer so that we can say, as he did, 'Father, I know that you always hear me.'

In focusing on the knowledge of God the Son we have acknowledged that real distinctions exist between the three persons of the Trinity. In doing so we also have to realize that knowing the Son is to know him as the Spirit-indwelt Son of the Father. The gospel is primarily about the work of the Son. How we know the Son will determine how we view our relationship with the Father who speaks to us through his word. How we view that relationship will determine, in turn, how we come to God in prayer and with what confidence. Prayer will never again be a sentimental excursion or an instinctive hitting of the panic button. Nor will it be the presumption of an innate right to demand God's attention. Rather it will be the expression of our entry into God's heavenly sanctuary, which has been procured for us by our Great High Priest.

> Therefore, brothers, since we have confidence to enter the holy places by the blood of Jesus, by the new and living way that he opened for us through the

> curtain, that is, through his flesh, and since we have a great priest over the house of God, let us draw near with a true heart in full assurance of faith, with our hearts sprinkled clean from an evil conscience and our bodies washed with pure water.
>
> (Heb. 10:19–23)

Summary

- Jesus is the only true (human) son of the Father.
- Prayer belongs to the sons of the Father, but we have repudiated that relationship by our sin.
- As the true son, Jesus calls to the Father with the confidence that he is always heard.
- When we are united to Christ by faith we receive true sonship in him, and we can consequently pray with the same confidence that we are heard.

Pause a moment . . .

Consider again the real basis of our confidence that God hears our prayers. When the doubts about this assail you, do you think mainly about:

- how faithful and good a praying person you are, or
- how faithful and acceptable to God Jesus was on our behalf?

Have you pondered how central to the gospel our justification by faith is, and how this relates to prayer?

4 The source of all prayer

Who changes what through prayer?

The popular refrain that 'prayer changes things' bears examination. Not that I want to sound like a sceptic, because there is little doubt about the truth of this statement when it is rightly understood. The question for us is, 'Who changes what through prayer?' I began this study by looking at the fact that God is the speaking God who spoke the universe into being, and who spoke to those created in his image, setting out ground rules and establishing the framework within which we live and think before God. This brings us to the subject of the sovereignty of God. Amongst evangelical Christians the fact of God's rulership over all things finds basic agreement. There are, however, some wide-ranging disagreements about how this divine rulership is exercised and how it relates to us as choice-making creatures.

These disagreements inevitably flow on into our understanding of the way in which our prayer relates to the sovereign will of God. Some might pose the question thus: 'What is the point in praying to God if everything has been determined beforehand?' The implication of this question is that there is no point in praying if we cannot change God's mind, or at least influence it in some way, by praying. The obvious rejoinder is: 'What is the point in praying to God if he is not in control of all things?' In other words, if the matter is not in God's department, either because he has surrendered control or because he never had control, then there is little point is asking him to do something about it.

Let us consider the common view of prayer that somehow we can induce God to change his mind if only we can get it right at our end. In addressing the subject of prayer and the sovereignty of God, Arthur Pink wrote, 'In the great majority of books written, and in the sermons preached upon prayer, the human element fills the scene almost entirely: it is the conditions which *we* must meet, the promises *we* must claim, the things *we* must do, in order to get our requests granted; and *God's* claims, *God's* right, *God's* glory are often disregarded.'[1] Pink rightly points out that we must come to the subject from the reality of God and then try to understand how we fit into that reality. The question is really a specific form of the general consideration of how God can be sovereign if we as human beings make real choices. I prefer not to frame this in terms of our having 'free will' since this is not a biblical notion and needs too much qualifying to take account of our sinful nature. Remember that when the humanist scholar Erasmus wrote his treatise on the freedom of the will, Martin Luther replied with his treatise on the bondage of the will. The reality and extent of this bondage is related to this problem of divine sovereignty and human responsibility. Even as Christians we need to take into account the effect that our continuing sinfulness has on our wills.

Human logic argues that once we accept that choice-making is an expression of a truly free will, then we are bound to accept some kind of self-limitation, or even forced limitation, of the sovereignty of God. This hardly fits the evidence of Scripture. Even allowing for the liberty we have in the gospel, we continue to battle against our sinful nature. The problem is still more basic, for it involves the relationship of God's sovereignty to our responsibility in choice making. While the will is not free because of sin, we remain responsible. But if we assume that human responsibility somehow limits the way God can

---

1. A. W. Pink, *The Sovereignty of God* (Edinburgh: Banner of Truth, 1961), p. 109.

exercise his sovereign will, then he is no longer sovereign. Again human logic sees it as an 'either-or' matter. Furthermore, the same 'either-or' logic when applied to Jesus and to God puts us in a real bind. If Jesus is fully God, this logic would decree that he cannot be at the same time fully man. By the same logic, if God is one God, he cannot at the same time be three persons. Now, consider the idea that prayer starts with us, somehow influences God, and then produces some outcome. This approach comes out of a concern to preserve human freedom and responsibility but senses that it can only do so by limiting God's sovereignty. Yet surely it is no more difficult to accommodate human responsibility with divine sovereignty than it is to accept the fact that God is Trinity or that Jesus is two natures in one person. They are all beyond our human capacity to understand, but not beyond us to accept as what God's word teaches.

The popular, unreflective view on prayer seems to concentrate on our activity as praying people. That is why it is reasoned that we must stir people up to pray with all kinds of incentives. We might represent this view in a diagram thus:

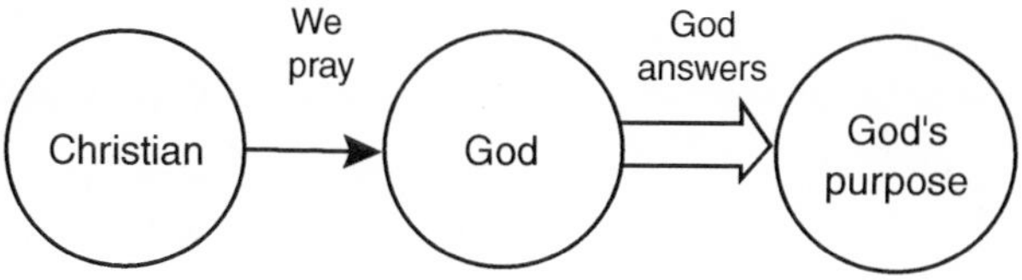

Diagram 1: Popular perspective on prayer

According to this view, prayer is something that we essentially initiate. On whatever basis, we decide that it is a good thing to pray for certain goals to be achieved. No one would suggest that what we pray for is not guided to some degree by considerations of the will of God, but the activity of prayer is seen to be the way that we somehow influence the outcome. It is as if God either will not or cannot act until Christians get on with the business of praying that he will so act. Thus, we pray, and this causes God to act by way of an answer and to fulfil his purposes. Some would go further than this and link the outcome more with the quality or strength of our faith than with any specific revealed purpose of God. We will consider some aspects of that emphasis in the next chapter.

There is enough truth in the view represented in the diagram above to make it attractive. Of course there is an important role for human responsibility and for encouragements to pray.[2] The problem lies in the fact that it fosters the notion of the impotence of God to act unless we get on with the business of praying. If prayer changes things, then we have to accept, on this view, that it changes God from being inactive to active. Some might even suggest it changes him from being unwilling to being willing to act. This is a perspective that is misleading because it all but ignores the role that God's sovereign plan, his revelation and his Spirit have in initiating prayer. By focusing almost entirely on our responsibility to pray, an 'either-or' logic takes over and undermines the biblical perspective. If God as Trinity is a 'both-and' reality (that is, he is both one God and three persons), in the same way that Jesus as the God-Man is 'both-and' (that is, he is both sovereign God and responsible human), then we must be prepared for that kind of reality to be generally in evidence in God's world. This would be expected most of all in the matter of our relationship to God, since the two natures of Jesus exemplify the relationship of deity and humanity. Because prayer is but one aspect of our relationship as responsible humans to the sovereign God, we should expect it to be a function of both God's sovereignty and our responsible action. This, in fact, is what we find the biblical evidence points to.

How a sovereign God relates to responsible humanity

It is vital that we should be aware of the problems created by human 'either-or' logic. Of course some situations are clearly 'either-or'. We are either male or female. The Bible reminds us that 'God is light, and in him is no darkness at all' (1 John 1:5). But there are other times where the Bible indicates that we have to cope with a 'both-and' situation. We have seen this, above all, in the person of God and in Jesus. Yet, the 'both-and' logic doesn't always come easily to us. For

---

2. So Hebrews 10:24 indicates that we should 'consider how to stir up one another to love and good works'.

example, if we stress the sovereignty of God in salvation, some people will take this to mean that we, as humans, are simply robots or puppets on a string. If we say that God, the sovereign Lord, initiates prayer, there are some who will read this as meaning that we have no responsibility in the matter. This clearly does not follow. It is worth pondering the point that our responsibility is actually a derivative of God's sovereignty. If he were not totally sovereign, then it is difficult to see how he could give us total responsibility. Responsibility implies an authority before which and to which we are responsible. The idea of free will is that it is totally subjective and self-generating. Responsibility, by contrast, is a response to some objective and external authority.

Let us think about this 'both-and' perspective further. The doctrine of the Trinity states, without in any way solving the mystery of how it can be, that God is both one God *and* three persons. Calling the three persons Father, Son and Holy Spirit is not merely a way of referring to God's different roles as Creator, Redeemer and Sanctifier, but expresses the reality of God's being. Thus, if he had never created, and if there had never been any sinners to redeem or to sanctify, God would still be, from eternity to eternity, Father, Son and Holy Spirit.[3] When it comes to the person of Christ, the same kind of relationship exists between his divine and human natures. In Jesus, however, we have the clearest and most perfect expression of how God relates to humanity. God remains sovereign God, and man remains responsible man. Furthermore, Jesus can be seen as the most perfectly integrated personality that has ever existed. There is absolutely no conflict between his sovereign deity and his responsible humanity. This is important, not only for understanding prayer, but also for understanding the whole of our existence as the people of God. The way to avoid the error is not to understand *how* the 'both-and' can exist, but

---

3. In technical terms, we distinguish between the *ontological* Trinity (what God is in his being) and the *economic* Trinity (what God is like in his actions; the distinctions between the three persons are made in terms of what each primarily does, such as create, redeem and sanctify). Such distinctions between the persons of the Trinity should never be allowed to overshadow the oneness of God.

to accept *that* they exist and to ensure that we give equal weight to both perspectives. This is not the same as saying that we balance the two truths. Balance is not a helpful word here because it suggests that God's sovereignty and our human responsibility are equal in all respects. They clearly are not. I prefer to talk about maintaining the biblical perspective on the matter.

This perspective in the matter of prayer means that we acknowledge our human responsibility to pray and, to that end, we will preach, teach and exhort one another to pray. It also means that we acknowledge the sovereignty of God in prayer, so that we recognize its nature as something that begins with God. While popular logic decrees that either God must be sovereign *or* we must be responsible (it cannot be both), Christian logic accepts that it must be both if the biblical evidence demands it. It is clear from the Bible that God is sovereign and works all things according to the purpose of his will. It is also clear that we are responsible to act before God in a way that reflects who God is and who we are before him.

God made the first move in salvation

Let us now return to the point that prayer is an activity of the saved people of God. It belongs to us because of the sonship that has been restored to us through the life, death and resurrection of Jesus. Learning to pray and developing one's habits of prayer is one of the fruits of our salvation in Christ. Furthermore, salvation is not only the process of our initial conversion and coming to faith in Christ. It is the whole process by which God brings us out of darkness into light, regenerates us, converts us, justifies, sanctifies and, eventually at the return of Christ, glorifies us.

It is important to recognize the sovereignty of God and his divine initiative in every aspect of our salvation. This is because of sin. Without in any way detracting from the importance of God's judicial sentence of death upon us as a race of rebels, there is a sense in which we ourselves have committed spiritual suicide. The result is, as Paul says in Ephesians 2:1, that we were dead in our trespasses and sins. In Christ we have been made alive, but we are still utterly dependent on the sovereign working of God. As we seek to let our salvation have its outworking in our lives, we are reminded by Paul in Philippians 2:12–13 that 'it is God who works in you, both to will and to work for his good pleasure'. Having been saved by grace, not by works, we are again reminded by Paul in Ephesians 2:10 that 'we are his workmanship, created in Christ Jesus for good works, which God prepared beforehand, that we should walk in them'. These passages are representative of the clear New Testament teaching that God's sovereignty and our responsibility exist together.

A non-Christian view of prayer will not take any account of the nature and seriousness of sin. God can be regarded as a kind of attendant at the information desk in the local shopping mall. When we feel that we really need something, we can saunter up and make the request. There is no barrier, no judgment of a holy God on our rebellion, and no 'great chasm fixed' (see Luke 16:26) between us, all of which need a saviour to deal with them. Heaven is regarded as a drop-in centre and, when we feel the urge or haven't got anything better to do, we can call by for a chat. Such a view may appear to be somewhat of a caricature, yet I think it is not far from many unconverted people's understanding of prayer. In any case there is the assumption that it is our inalienable birthright as decent human beings to pray to God or gods when and how we see fit. This is totally at variance with the biblical view of our need of grace.

A corollary of the biblical view of sin is the fact that salvation proceeds from God's undeserved love and grace towards us. Salvation is God's eternal plan that is expressed in his unilateral commitment to his people. In other words, God's acts to save us were done without our consent or co-operation. God did not call a committee of interested people together to discuss plans for salvation. Before the world was made he had determined to have a people for himself that would be saved by Christ. On this basis, God sovereignly makes covenant with his people, that is, he expresses his commitment wholly to them (Gen 12:1–3; Rom. 5:6–10). The divine initiative in creation and salvation points to the divine initiative in all righteous deeds. In redemption, God speaks his saving word to people. Thus, any word of prayer spoken in response will be a word that expresses either submission to Christ or rebellion against him.

In saving us, God reveals his purposes for the whole creation

In prayer we involve ourselves in the business that God has with the world. Even in uttering praises to God for who he is and for the kind of God he has shown himself to be, we are inescapably concerned with God as he acts and reveals himself in the world. We do not worship or praise or petition God in the abstract. If we go back to the praises of Israel, principally found in the Psalms, we will find that the praise of God is primarily for the great things he has done, because it is in his deeds that we know his character. More than anything, the overarching story of the Bible reveals to us God's purposes for the whole of creation. Christians recognize this when they pray. We will praise and thank God for his goodness as it is revealed in the 'big picture' of the Bible. We will ask him for things that concern us as his people who seek to make Christ known to the world. We recognize in our prayers that a day of reckoning is coming at the return of Christ and we pray with that in mind.

Let me put this in the simplest possible way. The Bible tells us that God has acted in the history of redemption to bring salvation to his people and to restore all things in a new creation. To put it another way, God reveals his character in the Bible by telling us how he is saving us and what he is saving us to (Rom. 8:19–23, 29–30; Eph. 1:3–10, 18–20). In fact, I would go further to say that the whole message of the Bible is about God's work in creation and in re-creation through the salvation brought about in Christ. The gospel event (Jesus' life, death and resurrection) reveals to us what God wills for all who turn to him in repentance and faith, and how the whole universe is involved. We do not yet see or understand the full glory of what is coming, but we can be sure of it (1 John 3:1–2).

Christians at prayer have only one option: to pray towards the fulfilment of God's revealed purposes for the whole universe. Anything else would be an act of idolatry or of total rebellion against God. All Christian prayer, then, will be oriented towards the gospel and its God-ordained outcome. We might wonder at times about praying for some of the smaller details of our lives, but we shouldn't be put off. Every detail of our lives is caught up in the purpose of God for us. It is not the matters we pray about that are the problem, but what we pray concerning them. We aim to pray in a way that is consistent with God's revelation in the Scripture.

Prayer is 'thinking God's thoughts after him'

It is sometimes said that prayer is 'thinking God's thoughts after him'. This is a useful way of expressing the fact that authentic prayer seeks conformity to the gospel. The idea of 'thinking God's thoughts after him' also helps us to deal with some of the problems that people have with prayer. First, it addresses the matter of who changes what through prayer. I have been at pains to make it clear that we cannot simply say that we somehow get God to change his attitude or his intentions through our prayers. The gospel focus on prayer, along with the biblical perspective on God's sovereignty and our sinfulness, surely moves us to say that God does not change, we do. However, it would be a mistake to conclude from this that prayer achieves nothing. It might be urged that, if God does not change, there is no point in praying because everything is determined anyway. This would be to fall into a grievous error as I have indicated in the discussion above.

It comes down to this: having revealed his purpose, God graciously allows us, as his dear children, to be involved in the carrying out of his will. He gives us the privilege of identifying with his will by asking him to do what he has already determined to do. God loves us to ask for the things he has revealed that he wants to give to us. This is part of the process he has chosen to use in order to carry out his plan for the whole universe (Jer. 29:1–17; Ezek 36:37; 1 John 5:14). If you compare Diagram 2 below with Diagram 1 you will see some obvious differences. God is represented as the one who initiates prayer in us by involving us in his revealed will. From our point of view, when we become Christians we start to view all things through new eyes. A world that we once saw as being empty of God is now filled with him and his glory. It is a world both under judgment and under grace. We grow in our concern that God's grace will be seen and experienced more and more in this sin-torn world. We are moved to pray to that end, not because we have come to the conclusion that prayer is a good idea. Rather it is because God has ordained that our praying will be a part of the means by which he will bring his purpose to effect. The diagram below represents the priority of God's revealed will, and that God is pleased to involve us in the outworking of his will as responsible, praying people. Generally he does not carry out his will without bringing his saved people into the process through their prayer. Of course, from our perspective, we are more inclined to see it in terms of our initiative to call a prayer meeting or to include prayer for this matter in the Sunday gathering. That is why we need to be reminded of God's perspective.

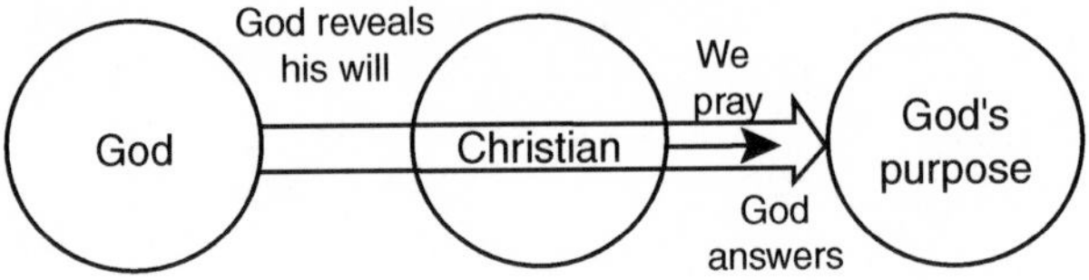

Diagram 2: The biblical perspective on prayer

There are some remarkable passages in the Bible that help us to see this perspective in prayer. While we can deduce this principle of thinking God's thoughts after him from all kinds of places in Scripture, there are some that are quite explicit.[4] The first passage to consider is in 2 Samuel 7. King David has just received God's promises through Nathan the prophet. These promises, the covenant with David, assure the king that the promises to Israel will find fulfilment in his descendants. David's son will build God's temple and will himself be the Son of God (2 Sam. 7:12–14). It is important to see that these promises make the descendant of David the focus for the fulfilment of all God's purposes that he has revealed, beginning with his promises to Abraham. In response to this covenant David falls to prayer (vv. 18–29). In his prayer he acknowledges his unworthiness, and he praises God for his greatness shown in his grace towards Israel. Then he prays that God will do the very things he has just previously promised to do:

> And now, O Lord God, confirm forever the word that you have spoken concerning your servant and concerning his house (dynasty),[5] and do as you have spoken.
>
> (2 Sam. 7:25)

4. I am indebted to Arthur Pink for some of these examples. See A. W. Pink, *The Sovereignty of God* (Edinburgh: Banner of Truth, 1961).
5. Parentheses mine.

> For you, O Lord of hosts, the God of Israel, have made this revelation to your servant, saying, 'I will build you a house.' Therefore your servant has found courage to pray this prayer to you. And now, O Lord God, you are God, and your words are true, and you have promised this good thing to your servant. Now therefore may it please you to bless the house of your servant, so that it may continue forever before you. For you, O Lord God, have spoken, and with your blessing shall the house of your servant be blessed forever.
>
> (2 Sam. 7:27–29)

It is inconceivable that David prays like this because he is nervous that God might go back on his word. David's prayer is confident, yet he petitions, in effect, 'your will be done'. If he needs courage to pray it is because he is aware that he deserves none of this good that God has promised.

A second passage to consider is found in Jeremiah 29. This gives the text of the prophet's letter to the Jewish exiles in Babylon. Before the exile God told the Jews through Jeremiah that his purposes would be worked out through the captives in Babylon rather than through those who remained in Jerusalem. Now he reinforces that point:

> Thus says the Lord of hosts, the God of Israel, to all the exiles whom I have sent into exile from Jerusalem to Babylon: Build houses and live in them; plant gardens and eat their produce. Take wives and have sons and daughters; take wives for your sons, and give your daughters in marriage, that they may bear sons and daughters; multiply there, and do not decrease. But seek the welfare of the city where I have sent you into exile, and pray to the Lord on its behalf, for in its welfare you will find your welfare.
>
> (Jer. 29:4–7)

Having told them that they must get on with their lives in Babylon, the prophet then tells them of God's purposes to redeem and restore them according to his promises. On the basis of this revelation, they will come to God in prayer:

> For thus says the Lord: When seventy years are completed for Babylon, I will visit you, and I will fulfill to you my promise and bring you back to this place. For I know the plans I have for you, declares the Lord, plans for

> wholeness and not for evil, to give you a future and a hope. Then you will call upon me and come and pray to me, and I will hear you. You will seek me and find me. When you seek me with all your heart, I will be found by you, declares the LORD, and I will restore your fortunes and gather you from all the nations and all the places where I have driven you, declares the LORD, and I will bring you back to the place from which I sent you into exile.
>
> (Jer. 29:10–14)

The only condition attached to this promise is that the prayer will be earnest, God-seeking prayer, the prayer of faith. This passage is all the more significant because on at least three occasions before this in the book of Jeremiah the prophet relates how he was specifically told *not* to pray for the people of Judah at that time (Jer. 7:16; 11:14; 14:11). This was because God had determined that they must be judged for their apostasy. The exile into Babylon was at that time unavoidable. The uniqueness of the prophet's place in the salvation-history of the Old Testament suggests that the main lesson we can learn from this is that authentic prayer follows from the revealing of God's will for his people and for the world.

One other passage to consider in the Old Testament is Ezekiel 36:37–38. This is part of one of Ezekiel's restoration promises given to the exiles in Babylon. In this passage (Ezek. 36:16–38) God promises to do great and marvellous things for his people in the process of redeeming them. One emphasis of Ezekiel's prophecy is relevant to our consideration of prayer. Redemption is seen here as God acting, not primarily out of concern for the lost sinners, but out of concern for his holy name that the sinners have profaned and brought into disrepute.

> It is not for your sake, O house of Israel, that I am about to act, but for the sake of my holy name, which you have profaned among the nations to which you came. And I will vindicate the holiness of my great name, which has been profaned among the nations, and which you have profaned among them. And the nations will know that I am the LORD, declares the Lord GOD, when through you I vindicate my holiness before their eyes.
>
> (Ezek. 36:22–23)

He goes on to promise that the nation of Israel will be gathered from the nations, cleansed, given a new heart and spirit, and restored as

God's people. Part of this redemptive process will be the prayer of the people as they identify with the revealed will of God.

> Thus says the Lord GOD: This also I will let the house of Israel ask me to do for them: to increase their people like a flock. Like the flock for sacrifices, like the flock at Jerusalem during her appointed feasts, so shall the waste cities be filled with flocks of people. Then they will know that I am the LORD.
>
> (Ezek. 36:37–38)

All these promises in the Old Testament look forward to their fulfilment in the gospel. Thus they show that prayer, even in the Old Testament, is towards the outworking of the gospel.

Prayer and the knowledge of God the Father

Standing in Jesus by faith means standing with him in the presence of the Father as sons and daughters. In the Lord's Prayer Jesus taught the disciples to call on God as 'Our Father'. We see clearly now from the New Testament that the right that any sinner has to call upon God in such a way is not derived from who or what we are in creation, but from who and what we are in the new creation in Christ. Knowing God as Father is only possible if we know him through the Son. Furthermore, to stand in Christ as sons is to identify with the will of the Father. The revealed will of God is the gospel and all its ramifications. Thus prayer, which is to identify with and share in this will, is always towards the gospel. The only thing we can pray for is that the gospel will have its outworking in all the aspects of our lives, the lives of others and in the world. Prayer is *not* trying to persuade God to so something he otherwise would not do. It is our being caught up in the purposes of God and the expression of this privilege as his dear children who know him as Father. We do not know God if we ignore his revealed will and its outworking through the Son. If we do not know the Father it is because we remain in rebellion against him.

In the previous chapter I raised the matter of inclusive language with regard to a Christian's relationship to Jesus. There is another concern about inclusive language when it expresses a certain philosophical rejection of the use of the name Father for God. There are those who want to substitute other names on the grounds that Father reflects an unacceptable patriarchal culture that demeans females. I must emphatically reject this move and point out that, far from removing sexism, it introduces it where it did not exist before. If we would know God the Father, we must know him as he reveals himself, which is as God the *Father*. If we reject his self-designation in favour of substitutes such as 'Mother God' or 'Father-Mother God' we are confusing references to being and role with those to sexuality. God is not sexual, and his being named Father includes a role distinctive that is the source of role distinctives in the human family. The biblical title is not an analogy of human family designation; rather the reverse is true (Eph. 3:14–15).[6] Other substitutes for the names of the Trinity that seek to avoid both Father and Son inevitably sacrifice the full range of meaning attaching to the biblical names. Prayer ceases to be authentic when addressed to a god or gods other than the God who reveals himself as the Father of our Lord Jesus Christ.[7]

Summary

- Prayer is an aspect of how we, as responsible humans, relate to God, as sovereign Lord.
- In prayer we respond to the reality of God who acted of his own will to redeem us.
- In saving us God also reveals himself as Father, and his will, his plan and his purpose for the whole of creation.
- In prayer, God allows us to be identified with the outworking of his will for all creation. Thus, to the extent that we know him, we 'think

6. See David L. Jeffrey, 'Naming the Father', in Craig Bartholomew, Colin Green and Karl Möller (eds), *After Pentecost: Language and Biblical Interpretation* (Carlisle: Paternoster, 2001), pp. 263–79.
7. It is clear that prayer addressed to any supposed mediator other than the Son of the Father, such as prayer to special saints, including the Virgin Mary, who are alleged to have an exceptional merit before God, is not authentic Christian prayer. Such spurious mediation detracts from the efficacy of Christ's work and his unique ability to be our mediator. It also lacks any scriptural support.

his thoughts after him' and our prayer is part of the means by which God achieves his revealed purpose.

Pause a moment . . .
What moves you to prayer the most:

- the idea of the power of prayer to move God to act, or
- the idea of the power of God who allows his dear children to share in his revealed purposes?

Does the revelation of God through his gospel affect the way you think of relationships in 'both-and' terms?

5 The enabling of all prayer

How does faith relate to prayer?

From time to time you may come across certain statements about the relationship of faith to prayer that make you wonder and maybe even feel a little guilty. Someone might say, 'Your friend did not recover from cancer because those who prayed did not have enough faith.' Or you are told, 'To qualify your prayer with "if it is your will, Lord" shows your lack faith.' Such observations indicate a not uncommon view of faith, particularly as it relates to prayer. Sooner or later we have to deal with certain biblical statements about prayer and faith that seem to lack any of the qualifications that focus on the will of God. There are qualifications, but these apparently relate to us: how we pray and with what kind of faith. Consider the following:

> According to your faith be it done to you.
>
> (Matt. 9:29)[1]

1. When taken in its context, this passage is clear: the blind men believed Jesus could heal them and, according to their faith, it was done to them.

> Whatever you ask in prayer, you will receive, if you have faith.
>
> (Matt. 21:22)

> Whatever you ask in prayer, believe that you have received it, and it will be yours.
>
> (Mark 11:24)

Faith is an important subject since it lies at the heart of our relationship with God. It is important because the Bible has a lot to say about it. Yet, even though it is constantly before us in Scripture, both explicitly and implicitly, we can still get it wrong. One reason for this is that people often speak of faith, even in secular contexts, as a good thing in itself. It is also frequently dealt with as if the central reality of faith lies within us. But whether it is faith in ourselves or faith directed to someone or something beyond us, it is *having* faith that is seen to be important, not the specifics of what or whom we have faith in. This view particularly suits the mentality of relativism:[2] it doesn't matter what you believe as long as you are sincere. Relativism, or pluralism, declares that faith in Allah, Mother Nature, Buddha, any of the gods of Hinduism, Jesus, or all of these, all amount to the same thing. Faith, then, is popularly used as another word for believing in anything at all, having a blind optimism, or even simply being religious (whatever that means). Even worse is the humanistic 'self-help' approach of believing in oneself. But this is far, far from the biblical notion. Constantly in Scripture the emphasis is on the object of faith. Indeed, it should be said that its object is what defines biblical faith. Rather than focusing on how strong our faith is, we should be more concerned about in whom we place our confidence and trust.

It might be argued that the statements linking prayer and faith in the Epistle of James are not very explicit as to the object of faith:

> If any of you lacks wisdom, let him ask God, who gives generously to all without reproach, and it will be given him. But let him ask in faith, with no doubting.
>
> (James 1:5–6)

---

2. Relativism denies absolute truth and says that truth is what is true for you (even if this is not the same as what is true for me).

> And the prayer of faith will save the one who is sick, and the Lord will raise him up. And if he has committed sins, he will be forgiven. Therefore, confess your sins to one another and pray for one another, that you may be healed. The prayer of a righteous person has great power as it is working.
>
> (James 5:15–16)

But the epistle as a whole contains many references that make it impossible to read James' view of faith as anything other than Christ-oriented. It is also important, then, that we examine the biblical view of faith in general and not just the references to faith explicitly linked to prayer.

As we do so, we will see that faith can be viewed from two perspectives: as a gift from God that is conveyed to us by the Spirit of God, and as a human activity oriented to its object, which is God. Both perspectives are valid and important. Recognizing both the divine and the human element in faith helps us again to focus on the nature of the relationship of humans to God through Christ. The 'both-and' perspective must be retained: faith is both a gift from God generated by the Spirit of God, and a human activity. The priority lies in the Spirit's role in turning our gaze to Jesus and in removing our enmity towards him. Without the sovereign work of the Spirit we could not exercise faith (John 3:8). At the same time we make the conscious decision to consider Jesus and what he has done for us (John 3:14–16). If we feel that our faith is weak and wavering, the antidote is not to turn inward and to try to generate more faith from within ourselves. Faith is not like toothpaste in a tube just waiting to be squeezed out. The answer to weak faith is to contemplate more closely what kind of trustworthy and sufficient saviour we have in Jesus. The error in so many evangelical testimony meetings and biographies is to create a kind of Protestant veneration of the saints. The examples of others *can* be rightly employed, but only if they turn us to Jesus; we cannot imitate someone else's faith, but the expression of it can direct us to their Lord! Biblical faith can be illustrated by considering the faith we would need when about to drive a vehicle across a rickety-looking bridge. We would not ask, 'Have I got enough faith?' Rather the appropriate question is, 'Can this bridge take the load?' Once we can answer in the affirmative, the question about faith vanishes. Faith is just there because of what we perceive about its object. When faith is lacking the antidote is not introspective self-examination but contemplation of the object of our faith: Jesus the Lord, our sufficient Saviour.

Praying in the name of Jesus

Closely associated with the idea of praying in faith is prayer in the name of Jesus.

> If you ask me anything in my name, I will do it.
>
> (John 14:14)

> Truly, truly, I say to you, whatever you ask of the Father in my name, he will give it to you. Until now you have asked nothing in my name. Ask, and you will receive, that your joy may be full.
>
> (John 16:23–24)

These particular passages occur in the last discourse of Jesus before his death as related by John. At the heart of this address is the promise of the Holy Spirit, who will take the place of the physical presence of Jesus once he is taken from them. Furthermore, the Spirit, as Jesus declares, is the one who will lead them into truth, testify to Jesus and confirm the truth of his words to the disciples. Asking in the name of Jesus will be a new activity for them once his character is revealed through his completed saving work. These passages about prayer, then, cannot be isolated from the whole thrust of this discourse. This includes the emphasis on the words of Jesus remaining (abiding) in the disciples:

> If you abide in me, and my words abide in you, ask whatever you wish, and it will be done for you.
>
> (John 15:7)

Though Jesus is going away (a reference to his death, resurrection and ascension), the Spirit will come and make the words and deeds of Jesus the focus of the disciples' faith and confidence towards God. To ask in the name of Jesus is virtually the same as having the words of

Jesus remain in them. In the words of Jesus, it is part of the Spirit's role to 'take what is mine and declare it to you' (John 16:14).

In the passages quoted above, the reference to asking in the name of Jesus is important since it points to the object of faith. It is clear that asking in the name of Jesus is not to be equated with tacking the verbal formula 'in Jesus' name' onto the end of our prayers. When the Bible says, 'At that time people began to call upon the name of the LORD' (Gen. 4:26), it portrays the early development of the line of God's people through Seth, in contrast to the godless line of Cain. Calling on the name of the Lord relates to a people who are responding to God's revelation of himself. Later, the prophet Joel takes up this refrain to express the response of faith to the God of Israel:

> And it shall come to pass that everyone who calls on the name of the LORD shall be saved. For in Mount Zion and in Jerusalem there shall be those who escape, as the LORD has said, and among the survivors shall be those whom the LORD calls.
>
> (Joel 2:32)

Peter quotes this passage in the preamble to his Pentecost sermon (Acts 2:17–21), and it is a fitting introduction to his evangelistic appeal. It is, incidentally, one of the clearest indications in Scripture of the appropriateness of prayer as the first response of sinners in the process of being converted and coming to faith in Christ. Paul refers to the same passage in Romans 10:13 and points out that none can call on him unless they have heard of him. It is not the word or name 'Jesus' that is appealed to, but the gospel proclamation of the life, death and resurrection of the God-Man, Jesus of Nazareth.

Most or all of the disciples of Jesus would have been brought up as praying Jews. Yet in the Gospels we find two interesting references to their prayer habits. The first is when they come to Jesus and ask him to teach them to pray (Luke 11:1). What has happened that people who had probably been praying since infancy should want a lesson in prayer? He teaches them a pattern that begins, 'Father, hallowed be your name.' There is really nothing in the content of the Lord's Prayer that is radically new for a Jew, though the form would perhaps be novel. This request for instruction suggests that there is something about the teaching and actions of Jesus that is altering their perspective on their relationship to God.[3]

The second incident occurs during the farewell discourse passages mentioned above when Jesus teaches them about praying in his name (John 14:13–14; 15:16; 16:23–26). These references to the name of Jesus would be taken as rather radical. On the one hand he teaches them to acknowledge the name of the Father as hallowed, and on the other hand he urges them to ask the Father in his (Jesus') name. Behind this lies the whole significance of name in the Old Testament. The first human act of naming another person indicates a generic characteristic of the named: woman made out of man (Gen. 2:23). When Adam gives the personal name Eve to his wife, it is again to indicate her significance as the mother of all the living (Gen. 3:20). In the fallen world of human wickedness, rebellion against God is epitomized in the Babel-builders' expressed desire to 'make a name for ourselves' (Gen. 11:4). By contrast, the chosen father of God's people, Abraham, is told that God will make his name great (Gen. 12:2). Abraham's response to the promise is to obey the call, to go to the land and then to build an altar and call on the name of the Lord. The name of God figures prominently in the revelation of salvation to his people in the world. This name is not a mere label of identification, because the identification of the Lord can only be through his self-revelation. Furthermore, this self-revelation is not in the form of a list of abstract divine attributes.[4] His attributes are revealed by his deeds of salvation and by the word that he gives to interpret his mighty acts.

So this God who will save Abraham's people reveals himself first as El Shaddai (God Almighty) to Abraham, but to Moses he makes his name known as Yahweh. This name, regularly translated as the LORD in our English versions of the Bible, is the name associated above all

---

3. We will consider the Lord's Prayer in more detail in chapter 6.

4. I would not quarrel with those theologians who list God's attributes as a way of setting out his nature and character. Such abstractions, however, should be seen not only as a legitimate way of understanding God, but also as being based upon God's redemptive-historical revelation. Some of the modern attempts to substitute non-sexist names for the names of the Trinity (see above p. 40ff) focus on perceived aspects of God's character.

with God's faithfulness to his covenant promises (Exod. 6:3–4). The honour of God's name is established in the covenant and in his mercy to save or redeem a people for himself (Exod. 3:15; 6:3; 9:16). When God saves the people out of slavery in Egypt, Moses' song of praise links the saving acts of God with his name: 'The LORD is a man of war; the LORD [Yahweh] is his name' (Exod. 15:3). The Lord's name will be in his angel that guards Israel (Exod. 23:20–21). More specifically, the people of Israel have the name of God on them. Thus, when Aaron and his sons are given the words of a blessing to pronounce over Israel, the effect will be, as God states:

> So shall they put my name upon the people of Israel, and I will bless them.
> (Num. 6:27)

But they have been warned in the third of the Ten Commandments not to bear this name vainly (Exod. 20:7). The NRSV translates it as: 'You shall not make wrongful use of the name of the Lord your God.'[5] The Hebrew verb *nāśā'* is the usual word for *to bear* or *to carry*, and is not at all the normal word to indicate speaking or uttering. This commandment, literally translated, says, 'You shall not bear Yahweh's name falsely.'[6] Thus, when his people show the character of God by the way they live, his name is glorified. Those who belong to this God are called by his name (Is. 43:7). When they profane this name by idolatry and are rejected so that they suffer exile, they are 'like those who are not called by your name' (Is. 63:19). Thus the name of the Lord is a name that can only have significance in the light of his gracious saving acts and his faithful promises to his people. It is a name that speaks of his holy character and his love for his people, as well as of his righteous judgment on all who profane his name. It speaks of his presence in the world to save and to judge.

Against this Old Testament background, then, we must understand what Jesus says about praying in his name. He has applied this

---

5. The ESV reverts to the more traditional and ambiguous 'you shall not take . . .'
6. The popular notion that this commandment refers to blasphemous talk is of course included in the scope of the prohibition, but is only one small part of its significance.

tremendously significant Old Testament idea to himself. All that God has promised to Israel now finds its focus in the person and work of Christ. Not only is he God whose name is the Lord, but he is also the true covenant people on whom and among whom the name of God rests. To pray in his name is to pray according to the whole process of God's revelation as it comes to fulfilment in the life, death and resurrection of Jesus. That is why it cannot fail, for God has promised that his revealed purpose cannot fail. All prayer that is uttered in the light of the gospel, and by which we identify with God's revealed will and purpose in the gospel, will be infallibly answered. The answer might not be exactly as we conceive it should be, but the prayer will be answered.

Faith is our Spirit-enabled response to the Christ of the gospel

Just as God's word to us is inseparable from the Spirit of God, so also our word to God is inseparable from the same Spirit. The Holy Spirit enables people to respond with faith and repentance to the message about Jesus. This has two dimensions: what the Spirit does for us, and what the Spirit does in us. Those who respond in faith are those who are born of the will of God:

> He was in the world, and the world was made through him, yet the world did not know him. He came to his own, and his own people did not receive him. But to all who did receive him, who believed in his name, he gave the right to become children of God, who were born, not of blood nor of the will of the flesh nor of the will of man, but of God.
>
> (John 1:10–13)

John tells us that when Jesus came into the world and to his own people, the Jews, they rejected him. Some did accept him, and these were those born of God. If there is any doubt what this means, it is clarified in the dialogue between Nicodemus and Jesus:

> Jesus answered him 'Truly, truly, I say to you, unless one is born again he cannot see the kingdom of God.' Nicodemus said to him, 'How can a man

> be born when he is old? Can he enter a second time into his mother's womb and be born?' Jesus answered, 'Truly, truly, I say to you, unless one is born of water and the Spirit, he cannot enter the kingdom of God. That which is born of the flesh is flesh, and that which is born of the Spirit is spirit. Do not marvel that I said to you, "You must be born again."[7] The wind blows where it wishes, and you hear its sound, but you do not know where it comes from or where it goes. So it is with everyone who is born of the Spirit.'
>
> (John 3:3–8)

This new birth from above, says Jesus, is necessary if one is either to see or to enter the kingdom of God. His reference to being born of water and the Spirit is almost certainly a reference to the promises given through the prophet Ezekiel of a cleansed, renewed and faithful people who will be saved (Ezek. 36:25–27). It should be noted that Jesus does not suggest that we ask for this new birth, but indicates that those who are born again by a sovereign work of the Spirit are those who believe in him (see John 3:14–16).

The Acts of the Apostles is an important book for understanding this role of the Holy Spirit in faith. In Peter's Pentecost sermon we are told that it is the finished work of Christ, who is the truly Spirit-endowed Man for us, which wins for God's people the gift of the Spirit:

> Being therefore exalted at the right hand of God, and having received from the Father the promise of the Holy Spirit, he has poured out this that you yourselves are seeing and hearing.
>
> (Acts 2:33)

---

7. This is sometimes mistakenly taken as an imperative as if Jesus commands us to be born again. The Greek word *dei* means *it is necessary* and is indicative. That is, Jesus tells Nicodemus that, as a fact, the new birth is necessary if we are to enter the kingdom. In the same way, if a government tells us that in order to qualify for a passport 'You must be a citizen of this country', it states a fact in the indicative, not a command in the imperative. It is not saying 'become a citizen', for it might just as well be implying 'you can never qualify'.

The context makes it clear that here the promise of the Holy Spirit signifies, not the promise *as* a promise, but the substance of that which had been promised in passages such as Ezekiel 36:25–27 and Joel 2:28–32. The significance of Pentecost is that the risen Christ shares his Spirit with his people. This gift of the Spirit is implicit in some statements that focus on the sovereign work of God in bringing people to faith. For example, when Paul and Barnabas preach to the Gentiles in Antioch, the outcome is described in terms of the sovereignty of God:

> And when the Gentiles heard this, they began rejoicing and glorifying the word of the Lord, and as many as were appointed to eternal life believed.
>
> (Acts 13:48)

In a similar strain we learn of the conversion of Lydia in Philippi:

> The Lord opened her heart to pay attention to what was said by Paul.
>
> (Acts 16:14)

This opening of the heart is the work of the Spirit. The human side of faith is seen in the apostles' response to the cry of the Philippian jailer: 'What must I do to be saved?'

> And they said, 'Believe in the Lord Jesus, and you will be saved, you and your household.'
>
> (Acts 16:31)

Faith, then, is an essential part of the process by which God draws us to himself and saves us. We would not believe if the Spirit of God did not remove our blindness and hatred of God's truth. The genuineness of faith is always defined by its object, not its intensity. From our side it is the focus of faith, our faith, on a sufficient Saviour. From God's side it is the sovereign act of his Spirit. Thus, Jesus speaks of believers as the Father's gift to the Son, a gift that is infallibly effective and has its final outcome in the resurrection from the dead.

> All that the Father gives me will come to me, and whoever comes to me I will never cast out.
>
> (John 6:37)

> For this is the will of my Father, that everyone who looks on the Son and believes in him should have eternal life, and I will raise him up on the last day.'
>
> (John 6:40)

Prayer is an expression of gospel-based faith

In the light of the discussion up to now, prayer can be spoken of as the Spirit of Christ within us crying to the Father (Rom. 8:15; Gal. 4:6). This is what Paul indicates in these two passages about the Spirit's role in prayer. Through faith in Jesus we are accounted as sons of God. The dynamic of this relationship is the Spirit of Christ working in us to believe in Jesus' life, death and resurrection as the only grounds for our acceptance with God. This relationship of sonship involves us in a personal encounter with God that we express from our side by calling on him as our Father.

> For all who are led by the Spirit of God are sons of God. For you did not receive the spirit of slavery to fall back into fear, but you have received the Spirit of adoption as sons, by whom we cry, 'Abba! Father!' The Spirit himself bears witness with our spirit that we are children of God, and if children, then heirs—heirs of God and fellow heirs with Christ, provided we suffer with him in order that we may also be glorified with him.
>
> (Rom. 8:14–17)

Paul says that the cry of faith to our Father in heaven gives witness to the fact that we are his children. To whom, then, is the witness given? Paul's words could conceivably be construed to mean that our witness is to others and that the Spirit is witness along with our spirits to this fact. But the context and the grammar of the sentence strongly suggest that he speaks here of the inner testimony of the Spirit as he witnesses to us. Our regenerated spirits cry out in genuine faith with a certainty reinforced by the witness of the Spirit of God that we belong to him.

This understanding of the Romans passage is born out by what Paul says in Galatians 4:6:

> And because you are sons, God has sent the Spirit of his Son into our hearts, crying, 'Abba! Father!'

For those who share the sonship of Jesus, prayer is calling on the Father through the power of the Holy Spirit who unites us to Jesus by faith. Once again we recognize the sense of confidence and certainty that Paul expresses about believing prayer. John Calvin echoed this sense of certainty when he said that prayer is the chief exercise of our faith.[8] Of course faith means faith in the gospel of Jesus Christ. Faith in anything else for salvation is self-delusion. God gives us, his children, all things through the gospel. The gospel defines our destiny and our inheritance; it defines for us the whole plan and purpose of God. It is inconceivable that we should pray in a way that is not defined by the gospel. All prayer is intended by God to be a way of sharing in the revealed purpose of God for the salvation of the world.

How much do we know of God's plan and purpose? The answer is that we know what he has revealed to us in Scripture. This means that we have a very clear picture of the goals and ultimate outcome of God's action in the world. But what do we know of the details? Again, we know only what God has revealed in Scripture. Many things are not given to us to know. For example, we do not know the time of Christ's return; instead we are told to watch and pray. We do not know who the elect are; instead we are commanded to make a free offer of the gospel to all people. We do not know in what way or when our own departure from this life will occur; instead we take each new day as a gift from the hands of God and seek to live responsibly before him. Thus, there are many details of life about which we might make prayer requests that seem to be God-honouring and gospel-promoting, but without knowing before the event how God will move in these matters. In such circumstances to leave it in his sovereign keeping with 'if it be your will, Lord' is entirely consistent with the biblical teaching on prayer. Contrary to some opinions, it does not show a lack of faith. On the contrary, it shows that we are prepared to leave the unknown in the hands of a loving Father, knowing 'that for those who love God all things work together for good, for those who are called according to his purpose' (Rom. 8:28). When we pray we are asking God to bring others and us to the goal

8. John Calvin, *Institutes of the Christian Religion*, Book III, chapter 20.

that he has revealed to us. God has revealed to us the big picture of our salvation, not the details of how he is bringing us to that goal. As we pray for the means to live in this world until the end (means such as safety, food, material needs, healing, etc.), we must be prepared for God's gracious 'no' while we trust him for the best. It is not faith to pray for something that God has not revealed as his will for us, unless we are prepared to submit to his sovereign action. We cannot, in the name of faith, hold God to something that he has not promised in Scripture.

Praying in the Spirit

In Ephesians 6:18 Paul tells us to pray in the Spirit. We need to be clear that there is no suggestion here that praying in the Spirit involves some mystical experience of ecstasy or trance. Some have taken such statements as the signal to bypass all the principles we have looked at regarding the revealed will of God in Scripture. We note that, in the passage in question, the insertion of a paragraph break after verse 17 in NRSV is not justified by the Greek text. This break gives the impression that Paul commences a new subject here, so that praying in the Spirit is not connected with what goes before. The ESV is more accurate, as verse 18 is connected to the sentence that runs on from verse 17:

> And take the helmet of salvation, and the sword of the Spirit, which is the word of God, praying at all times in the Spirit, with all prayer and supplication.
>
> (Eph. 6:17–18)[9]

Paul's exhortation to pray in the Spirit follows his word about putting on the whole armour of God. Praying, then, is part of the process of standing firm in the gospel. As Peter O'Brien comments, 'Paul wants his readers to understand that prayer is "foundational for the deployment of all the other weapons" and is therefore crucial if

9. The NIV also avoids the break found in the NRSV.

they are to stand firm in their spiritual struggle.'[10] It is also important to notice that the word and the Spirit go together. The word is the sword of the Spirit and the Spirit does not work apart from the word. This is consistently true in the Bible and has its basis in the nature of God as Trinity. The Word that became flesh (John 1:14) is not a separate word from the word of the Bible. Furthermore, it was not a part of the Word that became flesh but the Word. Thus, Jesus Christ is the Word, not a part of it. We know of this Word only through the Spirit-inspired word of the Bible. The Bible as the word of God has its authority, not only because the Spirit inspired it, but also because it is the Spirit's testimony to Jesus who is the Word. The Trinity is not divided: Spirit and Word work together to carry out the Father's purposes in the world. Some Christians want to plead for the Spirit without the word.[11] But the Spirit's role is to make us accepting of the Word.

Praying in the Spirit is praying in accordance with the revealed will of God in the word of God. The only way a person can pray, other than in the Spirit, is to ignore the word and to pray in a way that disregards what God has revealed. Prayer motivated by greed, by the lust for power, by selfishness or any sinful desire is not prayer in the Spirit.

Prayer and the knowledge of God the Holy Spirit

The Holy Spirit's role in the lives of God's people is clearly delineated in the New Testament. He is the Spirit of Christ, and as such his primary role in our faith and living is to bring to us the Christ of the gospel. In popular religion many things are claimed for the Holy Spirit that do not agree with what Scripture has to say. One of the dangers in the modern Charismatic movement is the tendency to separate the Spirit from the word. Our understanding of the Trinity ought to warn

10. Peter T. O'Brien, *The Letter to the Ephesians* (Leicester: Apollos; Grand Rapids: Eerdmans, 1999), p.484. The internal quote is from C. E. Arnold.
11. To avoid confusion, I have used lower case word when referring to the Bible as the word of God, and capitalized as Word when referring to Jesus as the Word.

us against this. It is a simple biblical principle that the Word (or word) and the Spirit are not divided. To claim that the Holy Spirit has spoken in a way that is contrary to the clear teaching of Scripture is to create an idol and to call it God. We can only know the Holy Spirit as the Spirit of Christ. He comes to make the person and work of Jesus real to us. The power of the Holy Spirit is the power that also resides in the gospel. The test of any claim that some word or action comes from God is whether or not it accords with the word of God.[12]

We have now explored the distinctive roles of the three persons of the Trinity in the reality of prayer. Christian thinking must take account of the way God has revealed himself to be: a communal being who is one God, three persons. The fact that God is unity and plurality is, as we discussed above, central to the understanding of the universe that he has created. The way three persons in one God relate is foundational for a proper understanding of all relationships in his universe. For our purposes it suffices to note that we cannot interchange the distinctive roles of the three persons, yet at the same time we cannot separate them. To put it another way: where one person of the Trinity is present and doing something, all three persons are present and doing that thing (unity), but we must give the emphasis to that person whose distinct role it is to do that thing (distinction).[13]

The question arises, to whom do we pray, on what basis, and with what enabling? The answer may now be put thus:

> Biblical prayer is prayer to the Father,
> through the mediation of the Son,
> in the enabling power of the Holy Spirit.

Is it wrong, then, to pray to Jesus or to the Spirit? No, because God is *one*, and where one person is present and active (hearing our prayer), all three are. But, and this is a big 'but', if we change the biblical per-

12. Notice how John links the testing of spirits with the gospel event in 1 John 4:1–3.
13. I am indebted to a former colleague, Geoffrey Paxton, for pointing out this useful 'rule of thumb' for handling the meaning of the Trinity.

spective by mainly praying to Jesus or to the Spirit, we will confuse the reality of prayer because we will confuse the persons of the Trinity. God is *three*, and the distinctions between the persons are not 'as if' distinctions but are real. If you look at all the examples of prayer in the New Testament after the ascension of Jesus, you will find only three involving a direct address to the Son, and these are clearly unique cases that are out of the ordinary.[14] In all other cases prayer is made to the Father. The pattern is beautifully expressed in Paul's summary:

> And because you are sons, God has sent the Spirit of his Son into our hearts, crying, 'Abba! Father!'
>
> (Gal. 4:6)

Summary

- Prayer is an expression of true faith that is defined by its object: the saving work of Jesus.
- In prayer we respond to the way God has revealed his name, that is, his character, as the God who is faithful to his covenant promises as they are fulfilled in Jesus.
- Such a response is possible because of the work of the Holy Spirit in bringing us to faith in God's saving work in Christ.
- To pray in the Spirit is to pray on the basis of our salvation in Christ, and to pray that God will work out all his plan and purpose revealed in the gospel.

Pause a moment . . .
When you reflect on the weakness of your faith, especially in relation to prayer:

- do you think mainly about what is wrong with you and your ability to have a strong faith, or

---

14. These are Stephen's response to the vision of Jesus (Acts 7:55–60), Paul's response to Jesus' voice from heaven (Acts 9:4–6), and John's prayer at the end of Revelation in response to the words of Jesus (Rev. 22:20).

- do you think mainly about what a strong and wonderful Saviour you have faith in?

What do you consider the relationship to be between prayer, faith and feelings?

6 The pattern of all prayer

The significance of the Lord's Prayer

The Lord's Prayer has held a unique place among Christians both in their personal or informal prayer and in the more formal prayers of 'church' or liturgy. And why not! This prayer came from the lips of Jesus himself. Of course, not everything that Jesus said to his disciples while he was here in the flesh is immediately applicable to us now. He said many things that reflected the situation of his disciples as they shared his company and anticipated the future as he portrayed it. He said things that applied to the Jews of his day in a way that they might not apply to us now. We need therefore to be cautious about simply taking the words of Jesus before his death and resurrection and applying them directly to our time. Much of what he said is timeless and directly applicable, but some is not. His death and resurrection constitute the definitive events of history, so we must now look at everything said and done before them as interpreted through and by them. The teachings and sayings of Jesus sometimes are more implicit than explicit in their references to his approaching death and resurrection. Two things must guide us: the literary context of Jesus' words, that is the purpose of the Gospel writers in reporting them, and the historical context, that is the overall significance of Jesus' ministry.

Having offered this caveat, I want to look at the prayer that Jesus taught. But we need to do this in the light of the completed work of Jesus here on earth. This prayer must be one of the most commented-on passages of Scripture in both ancient and modern Christian literature. In Matthew it is given as part of Jesus' Sermon on the Mount and not as a response to a specific request, as it is in Luke. We should carefully consider this sermon in the context of the Gospel as Matthew structures it before we simply extract it and apply it as timeless Christian teaching. Perhaps one key to this sermon is the assertion, 'I tell you, unless your righteousness exceeds that of the scribes and Pharisees, you will never enter the kingdom of heaven' (Matt. 5:20). This suggests that one of the purposes of the sermon is to refute the religious practices of some of Jesus' contemporaries.

The Lord's Prayer is given about half way through the sermon as a corrective to the prayers of the hypocrites who parade their piety in the synagogues and public places. The momentum of the rejection of a self-generated, works-based righteousness builds as Jesus goes on to urge them, 'Seek first the kingdom of God and his righteousness, and all these things will be added to you' (Matt. 6:33). This exhortation to seek God's righteousness, rather than their own, is surely significant. Then later there is an uncompromising warning that 'Not everyone who says to me, "Lord, Lord," will enter the kingdom of heaven, but the one who does the will of my Father who is in heaven' (Matt. 7:21). Whatever else the sermon is meant to achieve, it clearly functioned as a direct address to those Jews of Jesus' time who had come to rely on themselves and their doing of works of the law for righteousness before God. Jesus here 'pulls the rug out', so to speak, from under their self-righteousness. On this basis we can say that the Lord's Prayer functions in a way that anticipates the full expression of the grace of God in the gospel.

As I noted above, Luke's account of the Lord's Prayer is given in response to the disciples request, 'Lord, teach us to pray, as John taught his disciples' (Luke 11:1). Since prayer was a practice most or all of them would be familiar with, the request suggests that the events surrounding the coming of Jesus were perceived to bring a new dimension to their relationship with God. One theory indicates that in the Judaism of Jesus' time there had developed something of a loss of confidence both in addressing God as Father and in praying to him in the form of petition.[1] If this were the case, then the Lord's Prayer would point the disciples back to the more ancient traditions in which petitionary prayer was basic. We cannot doubt that Jesus taught his disciples in a way that truly anticipates the events upon which their relationship with God is established: his death and resurrection. In considering the Lord's Prayer, then, we need to do so in the light of the finished work of Christ. The language of the prayer is cast in a certain 'pre-Christian' and Jewish idiom, but this is a function of the fact that Jesus is with them in the flesh and that he has not yet finished his saving work. Thus, we find the New Testament prayers from the period after the resurrection of Jesus have some significant differences from the Lord's Prayer. In Acts and the epistles, prayer is couched much more directly and explicitly in terms of the saving work of Jesus.

In the Lord's Prayer there are some important new features that suggest that this teaching forms part of a bridge between the older traditions of Israel and the new age that is dawning with the coming of Jesus. This new age does not nullify the old covenant but fulfils it. It also shows more clearly the effects of the covenant beyond the people of Israel. The Lord's Prayer contains no direct references to the covenant with Israel, though it is totally consistent with it. Nor does it identify God in the historical terms of the old covenant, as was common in the Old Testament. Although many of the prayers in the Psalms are of an individualistic and personal nature, some of the great prayers of notable people are clearly framed in terms of the history of God's saving acts and the covenant with the forefathers of Israel. The prayers of David (2 Sam. 7:18–29), Solomon (1 Kgs.

---

1. The Jewish liturgy today, which has its roots in antiquity, does perhaps bear this out in that the overwhelming emphasis in the liturgical prayer is praise of God for his goodness and greatness. My source for this is *The Authorised Daily Prayer Book of the United Hebrew Congregations of the British Empire*, revised edition, with commentary by J. H. Hertz, Chief Rabbi (London: Shapiro Vallentine, 1947).

8:22–53), Ezra (Ezra 9:5–15; Neh. 9:6–37), Nehemiah (Neh. 1:4–11) and Daniel (Dan. 9:1–19) all show this consciousness that their prayers only have meaning as a response to the revealed grace of God in the covenant.

Now the gospel event is about to fulfil the old covenant, and the teachings of Jesus point towards this fulfilment. In the previous chapters we have examined the nature of prayer in the light of this finished saving work of Christ. The points that I have set out to establish thus far can be summarized as follows:

- The reality of prayer stems from our being created in the image of God who is a Trinity of divine persons that speak and communicate within the unity of the Godhead.
- The basis of our prayer is Jesus' sonship of the Father that we share in through our faith-union with Jesus.
- The source of prayer is the revealed will of the Father as we now have it in the Bible.
- The enabling of prayer is the Holy Spirit's gracious work of uniting us to Christ by faith and giving us confidence in the work of Christ and the word of God.

There is some dispute about the exact form of the Lord's Prayer, particularly in the longer version given in Matthew 6. This is indicated in the marginal notes in the English versions of the Bible. The commonly accepted version, including the longer ending, is consistent with the teachings of Jesus and the wider teaching of the New Testament. Using this form of the Lord's Prayer we can say that it falls naturally into a number of sections that we will examine in turn:

Address	Our Father in heaven,
Ascription	hallowed be your name.
General petitions	Your kingdom come. your will be done, on earth as it is in heaven.
Specific petitions	Give us this day our daily bread, and forgive us our debts,

as we also have forgiven our debtors.
And lead us not into temptation,
but deliver us from evil.

Doxology For yours is the kingdom and the power
and the glory, forever.
Amen.

The address: God our Father

Calling God Father was not a common feature of the worship of the people of the Old Testament.[2] This was true even though it would be a natural implication of God's referring to Israel as his son. We saw in chapter 5 that at that stage God does not reveal *Father* as his name but rather gives his people the name Yahweh (the LORD) by which to know him. The emphasis in the early history of Israel is on Abraham as the father of Israel. God is 'The God of your father, the God of Abraham, the God of Isaac, and the God of Jacob' (Gen. 3:6). But Israel is also the son of God (Exod. 4:22; Hos. 11:1), a notion, which as we have already seen, has important implications for identifying Jesus as the Son of God. The process of revelation, which climaxes in the declaration of Jesus as Son of God, includes the identification of Israel as God's son. In the progress of Israel's history, this relationship of the whole nation to Yahweh comes to be focused on the king, particularly on the son of David (2 Sam. 7:14). The king represents the whole nation before God. In the Gospels, Jesus is shown to be the one who fulfils the role of Israel and its king. He is also the son of David. Thus he, and he alone, can be identified as the Son of God in this human sense. Jesus, and only Jesus, has the right to call God his Father.

That God is 'Father in heaven' also has its Old Testament background. Initially heaven simply refers to the expanse that was perceived as being above the earth; the sky and the heavenly bodies in

2. God is referred to as Father or as the father of Israel in Deut. 32:6; Is. 63:16; 64:8; Jer. 3:4; 31:9; Mal. 1:6; 2:10. The metaphor of human fatherhood applied to God is seen in Pss. 68:5; 103:13; Prov. 3:12.

it. God was spoken of as being there because he was, as we would now say, transcendent. This means that, although he was thought of as being involved in the world, he was not tied to this world but was above it. From his position of transcendence he acts upon the world as one who is distinct from it. God rains fire down from heaven in judgment, but also rains bread from heaven to sustain his people in the wilderness. Heaven thus indicated a realm beyond the reach of people on earth. It was the abode of God and the realm of angels. God's dealings with his people on earth, however, were not the acts of a remote and unapproachable God, for he also revealed his dwelling among his people.[3] The tabernacle in the wilderness and the temple in Jerusalem were prescribed by God to show his presence among them. The danger of this was that a wayward people would seek to domesticate God, and this is what happened from time to time in the history of Israel. Solomon recognized that the temple was only a symbol and that heaven was the true dwelling of God. As he dedicates the temple in Jerusalem, he prays that God would 'hear in heaven your dwelling place' (1 Kgs. 8:39, 43, 49). The Lord declares through the prophet Isaiah:

> Heaven is my throne,
> and the earth is my footstool;
> what is the house that you would build for me,
> and what is the place of my rest?
>
> (Is. 66:1)

The word heaven, then, has two meanings in the Bible. It is that realm of creation that was perceived to be beyond the reaches of the inhabitants of the earth: the sun, moon and stars. Thus when the prophet speaks of a time when there will be new heavens and a new earth (Is. 65:17) he is simply saying that the whole of creation will be renewed. But heaven is also the abode of God and the place from which God acts to effect his purposes on earth. When we address

---

3. God is thus both transcendent and immanent. His immanence is not a fusing of the being of God and the world as pantheism teaches, but a divine condescension to be constantly involved in the created order.

God as being 'in heaven' we acknowledge his being distinct from the world of nature. He is over and beyond the world and is thus not subject to the laws of nature in this world. It is a way of saying that God is Creator, and sovereign Lord over all things.

The ascription: God's name hallowed

Most people, if they understand the word hallow today, would do so because they have some acquaintance with the Lord's Prayer. It is not a word we use in common speech. Its popular use in the composite form Halloween has associations with the very opposite of its significance that obscure the real meaning. In Halloween the practice of 'trick or treat' has trivialized the powers of evil and paganized the original significance that was given to the eve of All Saints' Day. The word hallow means to make holy or to honour as holy.[4] The phrase 'hallowed be your name' is an acknowledgement of the character of God. But in repeating this phrase, do we express what actually is the case (the indicative: your name is hallowed), what should be the case (the imperative: get your name hallowed), or what we desire would be the case (the subjunctive: if only your name were hallowed)? The grammar of the Greek involves a verb in the imperative, normally a demand. But of whom do we make the demand? Are we telling God to be hallowed? Perhaps we are helped by the fact that in the general petitions to follow the verbs are also in the imperative, a form normally used in commands. This would suggest that it is a petition.

If we allow that this prayer comes in the context of the fulfilling of the promises of God given by the prophets in Old Testament times, then we will recognize that responses to the covenant promises of God can express more than one thing. If God has promised through the prophets that his name will be hallowed and glorified with the coming of the kingdom, and if Jesus declares that this kingdom is now 'at hand', then the prayer response of the believer is at one and the same time an expression of fact (your name is indeed hallowed

---

4. The Greek of Matt. 6:9 uses an aorist imperative passive of the verb *hagiazō*, which means to reverence something or someone as holy.

now), a longing for this fulfilment (Oh, that your name would be hallowed in the world), and a respectful demand that the promise be delivered (bring glory to your name). It is not the Greek grammar alone that determines the meaning, though we have to say that the form of these verbs is consistent with this plurality of meanings. Rather it is the whole framework within which the prayer is given and the kind of promissory words and acts to which the prayer is a response.

The general petitions: the coming of the kingdom

The first of these two general petitions using the imperative of the verb is 'Your kingdom come'. Jesus had a lot to say about the kingdom of God, which he also referred to as the kingdom of heaven. According to Mark he began his ministry with the declaration: 'The time is fulfilled, and the kingdom of God is at hand; repent and believe in the gospel' (Mark 1:15). Jesus came to bring in the kingdom of God. The name 'the kingdom of God' is not used in the Old Testament, but the idea is to be found everywhere. This kingdom is both the rule of God and the realm in which he rules. In the Old Testament this kingdom was revealed as God dwelling with his people Israel in the land he gives to them. But as we come to the New Testament, even the land is seen to find its true fulfilment in the person of Jesus. The rule of God is through Jesus and its location is where Jesus is.[5]

The prayer for God's kingdom to come implies that it is still future. But in what sense? The kingdom of God is something that is both present and not yet present. Its coming is contingent on the coming and presence of Jesus. In fact, we can safely argue that Jesus is the kingdom in that he is both God and man in right relationship. He

---

5. I have dealt with this subject in more detail in my book *Gospel and Kingdom*, now published as part of *The Goldsworthy Trilogy* (Carlisle: Paternoster, 2000). See also my article, 'Kingdom of God', in T. D. Alexander and Brian S. Rosner (eds), *New Dictionary of Biblical Theology* (Leicester: Inter-Varsity Press; Downers Grove: InterVarsity Press, 2000), pp. 615–20.

is the Lord who rules and the true subject of God's rule. The kingdom can only be identified by the presence of the king and his people. Thus, while in the Old Testament the kingdom was located in an identifiable place of God's rule, such as Eden or the promised land of Canaan, once Jesus has come it must be looked for in him.[6] The kingdom comes in the present time through the gospel as the Spirit of Jesus brings people into faith-union with the King. The King will also appear at the end of the age to bring in the kingdom universally. Jesus' kingdom parables such as the sower (Matt. 13:1–23), the wheat growing among the weeds (Matt. 13:24–30, 36–43), the pearl of great price (Matt. 13:45–46) and the lost sheep (Matt. 18:10–14) all help us to understand this growing kingdom that comes through the gospel in the world.

Two things are inevitably linked with the coming of the kingdom: the salvation of the people of God, and the judgment of all who reject the kingdom. To pray 'your kingdom come', then, expresses an identification of the petitioner with the purposes of God in the gospel. We are asserting and, at the same time, requesting that this great saving goal of God will come to pass. To do this we have to identify with both the saving purposes of God and with his righteous judgment. We can do this if we realize that, biblically speaking, salvation is an aspect of God's judgment. It is not only saving those who trust in him, because he must at the same time judge all rebellion against his kingdom. We are all judged, but those clothed in Christ's righteousness are judged guiltless and acquitted. Once again we are reminded that the Lord's Prayer is not some universal prayer to be used on 'interfaith' or secular occasions, a fate that it sometimes suffers because it does not specifically name Jesus. It is, on the contrary, a clear expression of faith in the person and work of Jesus who is shown in the New Testament to be the one who brings all the promises of God in the Old Testament to fulfilment in his kingdom.

---

6. This is seen in the way the temple in the Old Testament is the focal point of God's dealing with his people in the land he gives them. When Jesus comes he declares that he is the true temple (John 2:19–22).

The general petitions: the doing of God's will

'Your will be done, on earth as it is in heaven.' Once again we must reject the notion of a kind of fond wish being expressed here. The whole background to the coming of Jesus is the clear declaration of God that his purpose cannot be thwarted, as can be seen in the word of the Lord given to Isaiah:

> So shall my word be that goes out from my mouth;
> it shall not return to me empty,
> but it shall accomplish that which I purpose,
> and shall succeed in the thing for which I sent it.
>
> (Is. 55:11)

This succinctly expresses the whole movement of the covenant of grace in the Old Testament. God's will is infallible and cannot be corrupted or subverted. God's will is to save a people for himself, and to bring in his kingdom in which his will is perfectly done. This petition responds to the revealed plan and purpose of God. It may be put in the broadest of possible terms, but at its heart it is very specific. The foundation for this petition has been laid in great detail in the promises of God given through the prophets. We have seen how God graciously involves us in the working out of his will as his Spirit enables and moves us to prayer for that will to be done. In that sense we share, through prayer, in the power of the word of God, not as some magical manipulation of supernatural forces but in humble trust in the promises of God that these things are indeed going to be. In thinking God's thoughts after him we share, not only in the thinking but also in the powerful acting of God that issues from his will.[7]

---

7. Biblical scholars have come more and more to stress the different ways speech brings about more than the mere giving of information. The idea of speech-acts helps us to recognize that speech functions to do things, that is, that it stems from a variety of intentions on the part of the speaker, and has a variety of effects on the recipients. The social context or historical framework in which a statement is made will largely determine how we understand the intent of the author and the effect of what is said.

Once more we have to see prayer as a response to the gospel and as a petition that the gospel will achieve its purpose.

The petition that God's will should be done 'on earth as it is in heaven' expresses the radical distinction between earth, the realm of human existence, and heaven, the realm of God and the angels. It is thus a plea for the renewal of the earth and all that is in it. It is a longing for the day promised by God through his prophets in the Old Testament. That day is the Day of the Lord when God finally acts to bring about the new heaven and the new earth. It is another way of saying 'Your kingdom come', and is explanatory of that petition. It anticipates the New Testament epistles, where this reality of the kingdom will be presented in such a way as to make clear both that it has already come and is yet to come. These 'now' and 'not yet' dimensions constitute the way the gospel works in the world. The kingdom has come in Jesus Christ since he was, as the God-Man on earth, the perfect expression of God in relation to humanity and the world. Now that same kingdom, or rule of God, grows throughout the world through the proclamation of the gospel. It is never perfectly here in the people of God because we are not yet fully delivered from our sinful natures. We press on towards that goal of sanctification, but it is never perfected in this life. Finally, at the return of Jesus, the kingdom will be fully and perfectly manifested in the world. All that is opposed to that kingdom will be put down and destroyed.

This petition, then, is a prayer that we, and all God's people, will live with our eyes fixed on the hope of glory. When Christians talk like this, there are those that suggest that such a fixation can lead us to be 'so heavenly minded that we are no earthly use'. I have occasionally met Christians who seem to come perilously close to this description. Mostly, however, we think of this description as prejudiced and unfair. In fact, it could be argued that the opposite is a much more pressing danger: that we can be so earth-bound as to be no heavenly use! But if the former can happen, what measures can we take to prevent it? I believe those most prone to have their head in the clouds are those whose view of their future destiny is less biblical than they imagine. Some Christians entertain a view of their personal destiny as dying and casting off a useless body while the immortal soul goes to heaven. Certainly the body dies and decays in the earth, and Christians universally believe that that is not the end of the story. But the biblical emphasis in the Christian hope is on the resurrection of the body, the whole person, on the day of Christ's return. Furthermore, this resurrection is a central part of the renewal of the universe.[8]

There are differences of opinion about what happens between our death and our resurrection on the last day. These differences occur because there is not a lot of clear information given in the New Testament. One view, probably most representative of historic, orthodox Christianity, is that at death the believer goes to be in the presence of Christ, and there awaits the full clothing with the resurrection body on the last day (2 Cor. 5:1–10). There can be no disputing that the New Testament teaches clearly the resurrection of the body. This is in accord with the final blissful vision of John in the book of Revelation. Here he sees the new heaven and earth, and the new heavenly Jerusalem. This heavenly Jerusalem is not a city *in* heaven, but comes *from* heaven and is let down onto the new earth. The biblical story has gone from creation to new creation. This new creation is different from the old but is not entirely discontinuous with it. Whatever the nature of physical reality in the regenerated universe, it will still be a physical reality, albeit transformed and renewed.

Thus, one antidote to becoming too heavenly minded ('pie in the sky when you die') is to reflect on the purpose of God to regenerate the whole universe. Our destiny is to live with resurrection bodies on a renewed earth in a regenerated universe. We do not despise our physical bodies because we know that they are not to be ultimately discarded as useless baggage, but are to be renewed and resurrected as glorious bodies. Likewise we do not despise the physical earth and universe around us. It has been made to 'suffer' on account of human sin (Rom. 8:19–23), but it too will be ultimately set free, for it too has been redeemed by the cross of Christ.

---

8. The emphasis on the immortality of the soul at the expense of the doctrine of the resurrection is forcefully rejected by Oscar Cullmann, *Immortality of the Soul or Resurrection of the Dead?: The Witness of the New Testament* (London: Epworth Press, 1958).

The specific petitions: physical needs

The framework we have examined for the general petitions also extends to the specific petitions. To pray for our daily bread is a simple recognition that we are physical beings that God has made to be sustained by physical means. It is a universal Christian practice to offer thanks before sitting down to a meal. We call it 'saying grace'. We acknowledge the fact that everything we have, our life and our sustenance, is due to the unmerited gift and kindness of God. That much is simple enough to grasp and most Christians would understand the giving of thanks before a meal in those terms. But do we reflect on the depth of that reality? It is something that should bring all people to acknowledge with thanks the good hand of God in the world. Paul, in Romans 1, sees the expression of human wickedness in the failure to honour God and to give him thanks, even though creation bears eloquent testimony to him (Rom. 1:19–21).

The background to the petition 'Give us this day our daily bread' needs to be understood. The beginning of the story of grace is found with Adam and Eve in the fruitful Garden of Eden. The redemptive story is as much about God's provision for people's bodies as for their souls. Indeed, the Hebrew view of humanity, which is consistent with the New Testament view, is that we are essentially physical beings into which God has breathed the breath of life. The term 'soul' in Genesis 2:7 (NRSV: *being*; ESV: *creature*)[9] refers to the whole person. The difficulty is that the word soul is used in a number of different ways in the Bible and it is not possible to assign a single meaning to it. This in no way detracts from the reality of the continued existence after death of what we refer to as the soul, but it is a reminder that the Bible does not see the separation of soul and body as a desirable or permanent state of affairs. The doctrine of the immortality of the soul, apart from the body, is an ancient Greek pagan teaching. The New Testament follows the Old in expressing the Christian hope as the resurrection of the whole person.

The significance of this holistic view of humanity is that we see it reflected in every expression of the purpose of God, and the good

9. These translate the Hebrew *nepeš* which is ordinarily understood as *soul*.

provision of God for his people. Originally it is the physical reality of Adam and Eve in the garden. Redemptively, it is Noah preserved in the ark with the animals. Covenantally, it is God promising to Abraham a land, a nation of descendants and his presence with them, and that they will bring blessing to all nations. The blessings of God are thus expressed in these down-to-earth, physical terms. A complication occurs when what seems like a straightforward enough plot begins to look like a dog's leg. Instead of going straight in and possessing the promised land, the descendants of Abraham end up in slavery in Egypt. Why this seemingly unnecessary detour? God could easily have made it rain in Canaan so that the children of Jacob need not have gone to Egypt for their daily bread.

The Egyptian sojourn and the subsequent release through the power of God taught Israel, and now teach us, a number of things:

- They show that, outside of Eden, people are not free to inherit the blessings of God. There is a barrier or gulf fixed between rebellious humanity and the blessings of God in his kingdom.
- They show that this gulf involves captivity to alien and hostile forces.
- They show that there is no release from this slavery without the intervention of God and his miraculous power. This release does not occur without a Passover sacrifice, the shedding of blood.
- They show that there can be no entry into the blessings of God, blessings that are 'earthly' and include the fruitful land promised by God, without such a powerful and supernatural redemption wrought by God.
- They show, through the events of Mount Sinai, that the redeemed people of God are to be people of the word.

The prophetic word of God at Sinai not only structures the life of the redeemed people in the promised land, but makes provision for the fact that the kingdom of God is yet future and that the sinful, though redeemed, people live by grace alone. The sacrificial system provides for the continual cleansing and renewal of the people. This system of sacrifice for sins is not simply a looking forward to the one perfect sacrifice of Christ, but had its efficacy in Israel because of its relation to that future atoning death of Jesus.

The prophetic word made it clear that Israel's expectations for the 'land flowing with milk and honey' could be sustained only insofar as they were faithful to the covenant. They had to learn that 'man does not live by bread alone, but man lives by every word that comes from the mouth of the LORD' (Deut. 8:3). It is obvious from passages like Deuteronomy 11 and 28 that fruitfulness and sustenance are not the natural birthright of Israel but a gift of grace. This principle is demonstrated throughout the Old Testament. Covenant faithfulness ensures possession of a fruitful land; disobedience invites God's wrath and an inheritance of captivity and wilderness subsistence. When we come to the New Testament, the fact that Jesus is shown to fulfil the Old Testament expectations for humanity and creation does not diminish the covenant-based and earthly nature of the kingdom. Indeed, if salvation consisted of saving our souls, as distinct from our bodies, it is difficult to see why Jesus needed to be a complete human being, body, soul and spirit, and to die bodily on the cross for us. The ultimate guide is the resurrection of Jesus, which was a bodily resurrection; the tomb really was empty! Although there were clearly differences in the resurrection body of Jesus from his pre-resurrection body (Luke 24:31, 36; John 20:17), there was also a clear continuity. He was recognisable, he was touchable, he ate, and he denied that he was merely a ghost or spirit (Matt. 28:9; Luke 24:37–43; John 20:27).[10]

'Give us this day our daily bread' stands in continuity with the whole teaching of the Old Testament about the physical creation, of which we are a part, and of the covenant regarding the provision of the promised land. Unlike the paganized enemies of the cross of Christ referred to by Paul in Philippians 3:18–19, Christians live as citizens of heaven (v. 20). These enemies have made their stomachs their god. They have turned the gracious preservation of humanity on this

10. Some modern theologians want to escape the implications of the empty tomb by arguing for a 'spiritual' resurrection, which presumably leaves room for the remains of Jesus to be still somewhere in the dust of Palestine. The Bible clearly teaches that Jesus lived bodily, died bodily, and rose again and ascended bodily. Paul's reference to the spiritual body in 1 Cor. 15:44 cannot mean non-physical. It refers to the imperishable nature of the body that is raised by the Spirit of God (vv. 51–54; see also Rom. 8:11).

earth into an object of idolatry. Our daily bread is a reminder to us that we are dependent entirely on the grace of God for our continued existence. We receive the good things of the earth as gifts from his hand. But we are thereby duty bound to seek the welfare of others and the preservation of the good things of the earth. Christians do have a responsibility to make governments and commercial interests aware that we share the good things of the earth only because of the goodness of God. Ecology, environmentalism and social concern should not be left to the philosophical greens and the worshippers of the earth mother. On the other hand, nor should it take the place of the task of making clear whose world it is and what he has done to redeem it.

Praying for our daily bread has a backward-looking significance as it recalls the way God provided manna in the wilderness and then brought his people into the land flowing with milk and honey. Finally, let it be noted that praying for, and giving thanks for, our daily bread has a forward-looking significance. Jesus linked the feeding of the five thousand with the manna in the desert. In doing so, he showed that these point to the 'bread of life' who is Jesus himself (John 6:25–40). It is not for nothing that Christians share a symbolic meal by which we 'proclaim the Lord's death until he comes' (1 Cor. 11:26). It is not for nothing that the New Testament speaks of the eating and drinking in the kingdom (Luke 22:15–18, 30; Rev. 19:9). However we conceive of the regenerated heaven and earth, and however we conceive of our resurrected bodies, the consistent biblical witness is to the regeneration of the physical universe and the resurrection of the body. One thanksgiving that used to be popular before fellowship meals expressed it well:[11]

> Praise God from whom all blessings flow.
> Praise him, all creatures here below.
> These mercies bless and grant that we
> may feast in paradise with thee.

---

11. An adaptation of the first verse of the doxology, usually sung to the tune *Old Hundredth*. Another version substitutes for the last line 'may love and serve thee faithfully'.

The specific petitions: forgiveness of sins

The lack of specific reference to the grounds of forgiveness has allowed this petition, along with the rest of the prayer, to be used in secularized contexts to signify some groundless general forgiveness of sins open to all. The background, however, is the whole Old Testament emphasis on reconciliation to God through the sacrificial means he provides. The foreground to the prayer is the direction of Jesus' ministry leading to his death on the cross. Again the prayer involves asking for what God has already promised to those who turn to him. If the Lord's Prayer is dependent on any specific and already existing prayer in the life of God's people, I would suggest that Solomon's prayer at the dedication of the temple would be a prime influence (1 Kgs. 8:22–53). Jesus cleanses the old temple because the house was intended as a house of prayer. He is the new temple that gives meaning to prayer. In Solomon's prayer, as in the Lord's Prayer, repentance and turning to God in prayer is a major emphasis. Forgiveness is never groundless but is based on justice and righteousness that has been tempered with mercy. The mercy is necessary because we can never satisfy the righteousness of God by our own efforts.

The second aspect of this petition is the linking of it to the reflection of our forgiveness in the way we treat others. The nature of the gospel is such that our reconciliation to God is real only if it is shown in the willingness to forgive others. Jesus' parable of the unforgiving servant (Matt. 18:23–35) highlights the fact that we receive mercy in the face of an enormous debt of guilt before God. Any debt that others have before us is paltry by comparison. If we receive such mercy, we must show mercy. This aspect of 'as we also have forgiven our debtors' indirectly speaks of the dimension of repentance in receiving mercy and forgiveness. To show mercy and forgiveness to those who offend us stems from the conviction that nothing that others can do to offend us can compare with our sin against heaven. This is even more vivid when the offending person is a Christian brother or sister. To withhold forgiveness from them when we know they are forgiven and accepted by God is an almost blasphemous placing of ourselves above God.

The specific petitions: deliverance

The final petition seems straightforward enough: 'Lead us not into temptation, but deliver us from evil.' The primary sense of the Greek word often translated here as *temptation* is to *test*, and so the meanings overlap. But while many people understand the connotation of being seduced into doing wrong things, the notion of testing emphasizes the need for steadfastness in the face of a variety of pressures to forsake trust in the Lord. In the book of Job, God allows the testing of Job when Satan[12] challenges the basis of Job's faithfulness and piety. This testing takes the form of incredible suffering, and throughout the book we see Job struggling to maintain his trust in God. He eventually emerges victorious. In Zechariah's vision (Zech. 3:1–5) Satan accuses Joshua, the high priest. Joshua is seen clothed in filthy garments indicating the uncleanness of the people he represents. Satan's accusation is implied but would seem to relate to this uncleanness. In other words, the accuser attacks the people of God at the vulnerability of their sinfulness. He throws doubt on the acceptability of the people before God. The answer here is the cleansing of the priest, indicated by his being given clean clothes with the declaration of the removal of guilt. The cleansed priesthood points to the pure and undefiled ministry of Jesus, our great High Priest.

In the gospels the heart of the matter is seen in the testing (temptation) of Jesus. Having been declared to be the acceptable Son of God he is then attacked by the accuser. Luke's account is revealing (Luke 3:21 – 4:13). Here the sequence is: Jesus' baptism and the approving word from heaven that identifies Jesus as God's Son; the genealogy showing that Son of God is the title that indicates Jesus to be the true Israel and the true Adam; then the temptation, which begins, 'If you are the Son of God . . .' Each test is countered by Jesus' appeal to the written word of God that had originally been given to Israel. In the final test Satan urges Jesus to play at being a superhero by throwing himself off the pinnacle of the temple. Jesus' rejoinder is from Deuteronomy 6:16: 'You shall not put the LORD your God to the test.' The implication is not only that Jesus would be

12. Hebrew, *haśśāṭān, the accuser*.

putting God to the test by challenging him to save a Son from plummeting to his death, but also that Satan's testing of Jesus, the truly human Son, is a testing of God who has declared this Son acceptable.

To return now to the Lord's Prayer, this final petition acknowledges the inability of the people of God to persevere without the grace of God. We are weak and vulnerable and, although Jesus warned of testing by the world, he also assured us that he has overcome the world:[13]

> In the world you will have tribulation. But take heart; I have overcome the world.
>
> (John 16:33)

We pray, then, for God to keep us from such a testing that will overcome us, at the same time knowing that he has promised to do so. We pray also that we might have perseverance to overcome to the end when the final and complete deliverance from evil will take place. Once again we see that prayer involves thinking God's thoughts after him, and echoing those thoughts in petition. It is a matter of coming to him in trust to ask for those things that he has indicated to be his good pleasure to give to his children.

In the context of the gospel, this petition is one that looks to our acceptance with God on the basis of the finished work of Christ. One vital aspect of that work was his human submission to the testing and accusations of Satan. The foreshadowing of this event is obvious. The first son of God, Adam, was tested in the garden and failed the test. As a result he, and all his descendants, were excluded from the garden paradise of God. That other son of God, the nation of Israel, was given a gracious opportunity to live as the redeemed children of God in the land flowing with milk and honey. This son also failed and found itself in the wilderness of exile. Finally, a true and faithful Son came into our self-imposed wilderness and stood the test, putting Satan to flight. He did this for us so that, when we are united to Christ by faith, we are accounted by God as having

---

13. I have dealt with the matter of tribulation for the Christian at greater length in my book, *The Gospel in Revelation* (Exeter: Paternoster, 1984), now included as part of *The Goldsworthy Trilogy* (Carlisle: Paternoster, 2000).

stood the test. That we are justified by faith means that we now share with Christ his acceptability with the Father. That is why for Satan or any human being to put us to the test is also to put God to the test: will he be faithful and save a sinner like me?

The doxology

The word doxology comes from the Greek word meaning glory and is usually employed to indicate some kind of liturgical praise of God and acknowledgment of his glory. As I noted above, this longer ending to the Lord's Prayer is not well attested by the manuscripts, but is in keeping with biblical teaching. It remains in common use in churches as the popular version:

> For the kingdom, the power and the glory are yours, forever.
> Amen.

This is a return to the baseline of prayer. Upon this basis alone can we approach God with our petitions. We acknowledge one God who is all-powerful and all-glorious. We do so, not as those on the outside looking in, but as those whom this God has graciously brought to his kingdom through the saving work of his Son. It anticipates that which is described in the vision of John in Revelation 7:1–17, where the people of God from the twelve tribes of Israel and from every nation of the world stand before the throne of God and before the Lamb and sing praises.

The final amen is a bit like the 'Yes!' that we exclaim when things go our way or we are in enthusiastic agreement with something. Amen is a Hebrew word that occurs in the Old Testament as a word of affirmation after doxologies (Ps. 41:13) or to agree with and identify with a prayer uttered on one's behalf (Neh. 5:12–13). The original Hebrew root provides us with words for truth, faithfulness and faith.[14] The way the word is used indicates some sense of certainty. If

---

14. Root meanings at best provide us with some possible indication of meaning. Context and usage must guide us, since word meanings can change and become quite separate from root meanings.

we translate it as 'So be it!', it is not to be read as a mere wish. It conveys a sense of inevitability when it affirms the revealed will of God.

Implicit in this doxology is the reality that we so often express in concluding prayer with phrases such as 'we pray this in Jesus' name' or 'through Jesus Christ our Lord'. The Lord's Prayer is Christ-centred and makes no real sense apart from him. Though it is perceived by many to be an appropriate all-purpose prayer for Christian and non-Christian alike, it was never given to us as such. It comes as an integral part of the proclamation of Jesus as the Christ, the Saviour of the world. As with the ethics of Jesus, so the prayers of Jesus belong only in the total message about the saving person and work of Jesus. In that context alone does the Lord's Prayer function as a pattern for our prayer. Most of all, the doxology should reflect our absolute wonder at the graciousness of God who allows us to call him Father. It should echo our longing for the appearing of his glorious kingdom, and the revealing of his power and glory. It can express for us the fact that, in Christ, we have a bridge between this mundane existence and the eternal glory of heaven.

Summary

- The Lord's Prayer is a pattern for prayer, but must be understood in its context of Jesus' redemptive ministry.
- Each part of the prayer has its background in the redemptive work of God revealed in the Old Testament.
- The prayer focuses on God the King, the coming of his kingdom, and what these mean for the subjects of the kingdom.
- The pattern of the Lord's Prayer demonstrates that all prayer is tied to God's self-revelation of his plan of salvation through Christ.

Pause a moment . . .

Have you become so used to the Lord's Prayer that praying it has become almost mechanical? If so, try spending some time each day reflecting on the significance of the main words and petitions of the prayer.

7 The progress of prayer
I. The history of Israel

The method of biblical theology

The Bible contains a marvellous unity within its diversity of literary types, authorial styles and emphases. Within this diversity we discern a consistent metanarrative, an overarching 'single story' that governs the direction of the diverse parts. By the term story we do not imply fiction, but the framework of historical narrative that progresses from a beginning through its climax to the end. The beginning lies in the creation story of Genesis. From here the story progresses through the account of the fall into sin, the covenant with Abraham and the exodus from Egypt. The story includes various focuses on the ongoing life of the nation of Israel until the end of the Old Testament. Conveyed through this narrative framework is a theology of the covenant and of the promises of God for the redemption of his people. The climax of the story comes in the four Gospels that declare Jesus to be the fulfilment of all Old Testament promises and expectations. The end comes with the promise of the return of Christ and the consummation of his kingdom as described, for example, in the last two chapters of the book of Revelation.

One aspect of the method of biblical theology is the retelling of the story to show its coherence and underlying significance in the revealed purpose of God to bring salvation to his people. Biblical theology is an approach to the Bible that seeks to allow the Bible's message about God to come through in the way the Bible tells it. It thus differs from systematic theology, or Christian doctrine, which sets out in some topical order the body of Christian beliefs based on the Bible. We need the approach of biblical theology to enable us to see the significance of individual sections or texts of the Bible for what they are. We need it to prevent us from falling into the prevalent error of using texts as springboards for sermons and lessons on almost anything other than the original significance of that text.

Given the nature of the Bible as 'story', it might seem logical for us to start the investigation into any topic in the Bible at the beginning of the story.[1] You will notice that, while referring to the beginning in earlier chapters, I in fact began with the New Testament teaching about God as Trinity and the significance of Jesus as the true Son of God for our understanding of prayer.[2] I did that because, as Christians, we can no longer come to the Old Testament as if we were pre-Christian Israelites. Our faith-quest for the truth of the Bible begins with our relationship to Jesus Christ. As individuals, we first begin to call on the name of the Lord as the truth about our salvation in Jesus takes hold of us. Our conversion by the gospel brings us into submission to the Christ who is consistently presented in the New Testament as the one who can be understood and known only as the fulfilment of the Old Testament. It is because of this that we need, and indeed desire, to understand the Old Testament, since it testifies to Jesus as the Christ, the Messiah. Thus for some there may be much to be gained in starting at Genesis and working through

---

1. Of course, not every part of the Bible is narrative, but every part fits into the overall context of the story. This is one of the implications of the recognition of the church that the Scriptures form a single canon or body of authoritative literature. It is not merely an anthology of religious writings, as some would have it.
2. This consideration of doctrine, in this case the doctrine of the Trinity, only serves to highlight the fact that, though it is necessary to distinguish systematic from biblical theology, the two are interdependent.

until it is becomes clear that Jesus gives it all meaning. Nevertheless, we no longer have the option to read the Old Testament as if we didn't know to whom it is leading, or as if Jesus had not come. We, as Christians, now read the Old Testament with the prior knowledge that it is about Jesus. We read it because he has indeed come. This will affect our grasp of the meaning of both the Old and the New Testaments in no uncertain manner.

Another reason for beginning with the New Testament is that it reshapes the beginning of the story by adding information to that available in the Old Testament. The Genesis account begins with the creation. But in the New Testament there are a number of places in which the writer refers to events 'before the foundation of the world'. One such insight comes in the prayer of Jesus as recorded by John (John 17). From this we are able to understand something of the discourse within the Trinity before creation.[3] Here Jesus speaks of the glory he had with the Father before the world existed (v. 5), and of the words that the Father gave to him and that he has now passed on to his disciples (vv. 7–8). Even the act of the Father sending the Son into the world (v. 18) is reflected in the Son's sending of the disciples into the world. The latter is not a wordless event, and we may infer that the former is also not wordless. Whatever the nature of divine speech is, it is now reflected in the human speech of the Word incarnate.[4] It is now possible for a Christian to begin at the account of creation in Genesis 1 with some sense of these events that took place before the creation.

We started, then, by looking at the subject of prayer in terms of how the gospel points us to the intra-trinitarian discourse that is graciously implemented in the word of creation, and the words of God to humankind that come to fullest expression in Jesus as the Word come in the flesh. Complementary to this approach of starting with the gospel is the use of insights thus gained in the course of examining the subject as it unfolds in the progression of the story. Biblical theology is a Christian pursuit and is carried out with Christian pre-

---

3. See Chapter 2.

4. We do not have to naively suppose that the persons of the Trinity have lungs and vocal chords for this to be a valid observation.

suppositions. Prayer in the Old Testament nation of Israel has its meaning for us now because of its relationship to the prayer of Jesus.

The beginning of prayer

In chapter 2 we looked at the notion that, before the creation of the world, God as Trinity was a discoursing God. The image of God in humankind is exemplified in the incarnate Word of God, Jesus. This Word and image of God is the faithful and true recipient of God's word and the true responder to that word in prayer. As those who are 'in Christ' (one biblical way of expressing our union with Christ by faith), we also respond to the word of God in prayer. As we do this we know that the weakness and sinfully tainted nature of our prayer is justified by the perfect praying of Jesus as our human representative. In other words, God graciously accounts us as acceptable in all respects as Jesus is.[5] Jesus, then, shows us that to be created in the image of God is to be created to pray. Such prayer is authentic only insofar as it is a response to the self-revelation of God in his spoken word to humanity.

With this New Testament insight into the nature of the Trinity and the divine activity before creation, we are able to address the evidence that we now know is based on this divine, intra-trinitarian discourse. Some of the Old Testament evidence that we have already discussed in relation to the trinitarian nature of prayer will be summarized in this present overview.[6] Thus, we have noted that human prayer comes as a response to the prior speaking of God. Authentic prayer is inseparable from the divine word that has interpreted both our humanity and the life that we lead. Adam and Eve were given such an interpretative word at creation (Gen. 1:28–30). By this word they knew the basics of how they should relate to the lordship of God, to each other and to the rest of creation. True knowledge is based on the revelation of God. The interpretation of every fact that mankind has discovered, or will discover, in this universe is dependent on this

---

5. See chapter 3.

6. See chapters 2, 3 and 4.

special revelation from God. The reason is simple. Only God has true and exhaustive knowledge of every fact in the universe and, consequently, only he can know the ultimate significance of every fact. This is not only because he knows everything, but because he determined and created every fact. The implication of the biblical view of the creation is that it is a unity within which all the diverse elements relate in some way to all others. They do so in accordance with the sovereign and creative will of God who is the Lord over all. He alone can interpret any given fact in relation to all other facts. The significance of this for prayer, as a response to the revelation of God in his word, should be obvious. If prayer is to be more than a groping in the darkness, it must be enlightened by God's revelation of himself in Jesus Christ. We must know the God to whom we pray, and be in fellowship with him.

In the Old Testament the verbal human response to God's self-revelation is first seen as God seeks a rebellious Adam in the garden. The rebel's response is one of defiance, self-excuse and the blaming of others. This rebelliousness is answered with the judgment of God and ejection from the Garden of Eden. In a similar strain, the murderous Cain answers with defiance to God's question, 'Where is Abel your brother?' (Gen. 4:9). Again the excuse is met with a word of judgment. We see here that God does indeed listen to sinners, but not with favour and acceptance. The prayer of the godless is shown to be defiance that invites the judgment of God. This may appear to be a harsh observation, but if people reject the salvation offered in Christ, they reject the justification of their prayers. We need to remind ourselves that God accepts the prayers of Christians, not because they are 'good and godly', but because Jesus himself is the true word of prayer on our behalf. True prayer is offered and accepted by grace alone. Goodness and godliness in prayer, as in every aspect of Christian living, is the fruit of our acceptance by grace. God justifies the ungodly (Rom. 5:6–11).

The grace of God towards sinful humanity is initially shown in the establishment of a godly line of people within which God is at work for salvation. Thus, in place of the murdered Abel, Eve gives birth to Seth. With the arrival of the third generation in the person of Enosh, it is said, 'At that time people began to call upon the name of the Lord' (Gen. 4:25–26). The contrast between the line of Cain, leading to a vengeful Lamech, and the godliness of Seth and Enosh, shows up the nature of real and unreal prayer. The latter is expressed by the defiance of Cain, while true prayer is found in the context of a family that is the object of God's saving grace.

From this point on, little is said for quite some time about prayer as an activity of God's people. We can only conjecture that there is a reason for this, since we know that people now do call on the name of the Lord. We find that the emphasis is on the way God speaks to his people rather than on the verbal response of those people. So God speaks to Noah revealing his intentions for judgment and his plans for the salvation of a remnant in the ark. This word is given to a man that, 'found favor in the eyes of the LORD' (Gen. 6:8). We are told that Noah complied with God's direction (Gen. 6:22; 7:5, 16). It may well be implied that when Noah was finally back on dry land and made an offering to God, he offered prayer with it (Gen. 8:20). But we are told only of God's verbal initiative in the covenant promise never again to destroy the earth by flood (Gen. 8:21–22; 9:1–17). Only in the pronouncement of blessing upon Shem and Japheth does Noah make an indirect petition to God:

> Blessed be the LORD, the God of Shem;
> and let Canaan be his servant.
> May God enlarge Japheth,
> and let him dwell in the tents of Shem,
> and let Canaan be his servant.
>
> (Gen. 9:26–27)

We shall reserve judgment for the time being as to why so little is said about prayer to this point. The reason for such silence may well emerge by implication as the story develops. For the moment we may suggest that the emphasis shows that prayer is not a conversation between people and God. God speaks first and all responses are responses to his authoritative word. We cannot speak until we are spoken to. Prayer is not speaking to God as such; it is rather a response to the God who speaks to us.

Prayer under the covenant

In his study of covenant, William Dumbrell has convincingly argued that the first use of the word covenant, which is found in the Noah narrative, formalizes the covenant relationship that God had established in the very fact of creation.[7] The creative word puts the creation under obligation to the Creator. Kevin Vanhoozer has pointed out that it is not only God's speech that is covenantal, but all speech. When we talk to others we are expecting them to pay attention, to hear and to understand.[8] Even if they fail to listen, this does not alter the fact that speech operates in a covenantal way by expressing a relationship with obligations. The covenantal relationship that the word of God sets up with creation and with the elect people of God is unique. We know God as the God of the covenant, and we address him in prayer as a reflection of our covenant relationship with him. To know him as the God of the covenant means that we must know what the covenant of salvation involves. The history of the covenant in the Bible is thus important for our understanding of ourselves as spoken to by God and as speaking to him in response.

It is perhaps significant that Abraham, the father of Israel under the covenant, is recorded as building an altar and invoking the name of the Lord (Gen. 12:8). The narrative proceeds thus: God calls Abraham to leave Ur and to go to Canaan. This directive is accompanied by the significant promise, subsequently understood formally as a covenant, that God would bless Abraham and his descendants. The promise of a nation, a land, the blessing of God, and the extension of this blessing to the nations of the world has in it the seeds of the whole biblical picture of salvation that will be unfolded in God's word (Gen. 12:1–3, 7). This is an important point, for we will note the relationship of prayer to these covenant promises. In this context we see

---

7. W. J. Dumbrell, *Covenant and Creation: An Old Testament Covenantal Theology* (Carlisle: Paternoster, 1984).
8. Kevin Vanhoozer, 'From Speech Acts to Scripture Acts: The Covenant of Discourse and the Discourse of Covenant', in Craig Bartholomew et al. (eds.), *After Pentecost: Language and Biblical Interpretation* (Carlisle: Paternoster; Grand Rapids: Zondervan, 2001).

Abraham as a praying man. Later, Abraham tells the king of Sodom that he has sworn to the Lord not to take anything from the king (Gen. 14:22–24). But the first recorded direct response of Abraham to God's word is found in Genesis 15:2–3. This word is significant: 'Fear not, Abram, I am your shield; your reward shall be very great.' This phrase, 'Fear not', innocuous enough on its own, is taken up in later prophetic words to the people of God as a formula for the assurance of salvation or of immediate deliverance (Exod. 14:13; Num. 21:34; Deut. 7:18; Josh. 10:25; 1 Sam. 12:20; 1 Kgs. 17:13; 1 Chr. 22:13; 28:20; Is. 10:24; 41:10; Jer. 1:8; Zech. 8:13; Matt. 14:27; Luke 2:10; 5:10; Acts 27:24; Rev. 1:17). Abraham cries out in despair since he remains childless. God reassures him that he will have his own son and a multitude of descendants (Gen. 15:4–5). Here the trusting faith of Abraham is affirmed, for 'he believed the LORD, and he counted it to him as righteousness' (Gen. 15:6). The praying Abraham is an Abraham under the covenant promises of God, a man justified by faith (Rom. 4:1–25). 'Fear not' is for Abraham indeed an assurance of salvation.

The prayer of Abraham in Genesis 18 presents the apparent problem that he seems to get God to change his mind over the destruction of Sodom. Had we received only this narrative in isolation from the rest of Scripture, it might indeed appear to be a story about a man getting God to change his mind. Two factors at least must qualify this: first, the overall teaching of the Bible about the sovereign will of God and, second, the frequently used device of speaking about God from the perspective of humans. Abraham is clearly being tested as to the faithfulness of God to his covenant. His haggling over the question of the righteous in the condemned city of Sodom stems from the covenant. Genesis 13 relates that Lot, Abraham's nephew, has gone to live in the region of Sodom, which is described as an evil place (Gen. 13:12–13). When some marauding tribal 'kings' or sheiks capture Lot, Abraham mounts a successful rescue. Abraham's intercession for the righteous in Sodom clearly has Lot in mind. The narrator tells us that, 'when God destroyed the cities of the valley, God remembered Abraham and sent Lot out of the midst of the overthrow when he overthrew the cities in which Lot had lived' (Gen. 19:29). Abraham also intercedes for a repentant Abimelech whom Abraham himself had deceived over his wife Sarah (Gen. 20:17–18).

The pattern of covenant prayer continues in the patriarchal

narratives of Genesis. Abraham sends his servant to find Isaac a wife from amongst his kinsfolk. This desire is generated by the covenant promise concerning Abraham's offspring (Gen. 24:7). The unnamed servant comes to his destination and prays that God will show 'steadfast love' to Abraham by granting him success in this quest for a suitable wife for Isaac. The word usually translated as 'steadfast love' when referring to God is a technical word that indicates the idea of covenant faithfulness.[9] The success of the mission is the occasion for the servant's prayer in praise of God's covenant faithfulness (Gen. 24:27). The patriarchal blessings upon offspring are also covenant-based and might be regarded as involving indirectly the prayer that God will fulfil his covenant promises to the new generation (Gen. 27:28–29; 28:1–4). Thus God becomes identified as the God of the covenant, the God of Abraham and Isaac. Later Jacob or Israel is added to the patriarchal band by whom God is identified. When Jacob fears the wrath of his brother Esau, whom he had deceived out of his birthright, his only recourse is prayer to ask God to honour his covenant promises (Gen. 32:9–12).

The Joseph narrative contains little direct reference to prayer. We see the aged Jacob in a prayerful wish to his sons over the demand to take his remaining son Benjamin back to Egypt (Gen. 43:13–15). There are echoes here of the plight of Abraham when he was told to sacrifice his only son Isaac. In both situations the covenant promises to the descendants of Abraham seem to be under threat. The narrative ends with Jacob and all his sons preserved in Egypt, far from the promised land. Jacob's blessings on his sons reflect either directly or indirectly the covenant promises (Gen. 48:15–22; 49:1–28). Under a king that did not know Joseph, the descendants of Israel find themselves subjected to an increasingly cruel slavery (Exod. 1:8–11). Captivity is not the salvation promised to Abraham! Thus, when they cry out to God for help, he regards their plight as out of line with his promises of the covenant (Exod. 2:23–25). That 'God remembered his covenant with Abraham, with Isaac, and with Jacob' does not mean he had forgotten it, but rather that he intended to act on the basis of

---

9. Hebrew: *ḥesed̠*. This word occurs repeatedly in the prayers of the book of Psalms, usually with the same covenant overtones.

it (Exod. 2:24). The entire Exodus narrative that follows is based on this premise: that God is a faithful, covenant-keeping God.

The prayer of Moses

As with all the great heroes of the Bible, we must be careful not to reduce Moses to mere exemplar of faith. Moses was a specially appointed leader who stands as the definitive prophet of God. That means that he is, above all things, the one who mediates to God's people the word of salvation. He is also a fallible and weak human being who is as capable as we are of offering God excuses for an unwillingness to be obedient. In Moses' case he was called to obey the command to be the saviour of his people. But the word of God from the fiery bush evokes all kinds of excuses, such as 'Who am I to do such a great thing?' and 'Who are you to be sending me on such an errand?', then 'What if they take no notice?', and finally 'I'm no good at public speaking!' This is not what you would call a good example of believing prayer! But it shows the humanness of the instruments of God's redeeming purpose, and it points forward to the humanness of the truly obedient Prophet that God would one day raise up. God has answers to all Moses' objections (Exod. 3:11 – 4:17). The emphasis of the narrative is on the word that God speaks through Moses to the Pharaoh. During this encounter the tension mounts and Moses finds it difficult to cope with the plight and mood of his people, who become more and more rebellious (Exod. 5:22–23).

When Moses does the rather improbable thing of interceding on behalf of Pharaoh, it is because he recognizes that the request has the potential to demonstrate ever more of the power of God (Exod. 8:8–15; 28–32; 9:27–35; 10:16–20). The king's repentance is superficial, and the end result is a further hardening of his heart and the emerging inevitability of judgment to come. As the story moves to its climax, the central point is the word and action of the Lord mediated by his prophet Moses. At the heart of it lies the final plague, and the deliverance of the Israelites through the blood of the Passover sacrifice and the miraculous parting of the waters of the sea. It is clearly the covenant initiative of God as Redeemer that is before us in the narrative. Moses must provide the most effective leadership, which is to call on the people with the assurance of salvation: 'Fear not, stand firm, and see the salvation of the LORD, which he will work for you today' (Exod. 14:13). The subsequent escape from slavery and the overthrow of the enemy is the occasion for Moses' song of triumph and praise to the Lord (Exod. 15:1–18). The specifics of this psalm of praise are important. In it Moses extols the defeat of the Egyptian by a Warrior-Lord and the covenant faithfulness of God, and recognizes that release from the alien slavery means the bringing of the people to the abode of the Lord. This abode is the place where God is pleased to reveal himself. Initially it is Mount Sinai, but eventually he will establish his sanctuary on Mount Zion. With Christian hindsight we recognize the convergence of these themes on the new Temple, Jesus, who is both the revelation of God's word to us and our acceptable word to God.

While Israel is encamped by Sinai, Moses functions mainly as the prophetic mouthpiece of God. The Sinai covenant is given to a people who are redeemed by grace and who need specific instruction as to the kind of life and national organization that is consistent with this redemption. Moses goes up on the mountain to listen to God and to receive instructions to relay to the people. In the midst of this comes a very great testing for the prophet. During his absence, the people persuade Aaron to make a golden calf to represent the God or gods who brought them out of Egypt.[10] This transgression deserves

10. The Hebrew word for God, *ʾᵉlōhîm*, is a plural noun that can be translated, according to its context, as either *God* or *gods*. It is, therefore, not clear whether the calf was in imitation of a pagan idol, or is intended as a visual aid to the worship of the Lord. Since there is only one calf, and since it is identified as the God of the exodus, it is likely that the latter is the case. This would still be to break the second commandment and to invite judgment in that any attempt to represent God visually is idolatry. This is because God has not revealed any visible form or likeness (see Deut. 4:15–16). Similarly, since the Bible tells us nothing of the physical appearance of Jesus, attempts to stereotype his humanity are open to the same danger of idolatry, even if not to the same extent (we may infer that Jesus must have looked like a first-century male Jew). Revelation, not artistic imagination, should shape our understanding of the Christ and his God.

the severest judgment. Moses reprimands them and offers to intercede for them (Exod. 32:30). So the prophet of God now stands before God and begs forgiveness for the wayward Israelites. His prayer comes from the burden of his leadership. He is even willing that his name should be blotted out of the book of God. This is a priestly prayer, one that foreshadows the role of the Priest-Prophet, Jesus, who will submit to the curse that is upon covenant-breakers so that they might be saved (Exod. 32:31–32; 33:12–16). Moses knows of only one ground for making such a request, and that is the covenant. The prayer of Moses is accepted; judgment falls but not so as to make a full end of the people. The tent of meeting is set up outside the camp as the place where Moses can converse with God and intercede for the people (Exod. 33:7–23). Once again we see prayer that reflects the word of God in true human response: the Lord proclaims his own character to Moses as the One who shows covenant-faithfulness and forgives iniquity (Exod. 34:5–7). So Moses has confidence to pray that God will forgive the iniquity of his covenant people (Exod. 34:8–9). Moses also intercedes for his rebellious sister Miriam (Num. 12:13).

Later, the people rebel because of the report of the spies sent into Canaan, and they refuse to enter the land when told (Num. 14:1–12). The threat of the judgment of God evokes from Moses another prayer of intercession in which he recalls the proclamation that the Lord made on the occasion of the golden calf. It, in effect, calls on God to be merciful and to remember his covenant promises. It is a prayer for forgiveness in the light of God's covenant faithfulness and mercy (Num. 14:13–19). Judgment and mercy are mingled as God decrees that this faithless generation shall not inherit the land, but that the covenant nation will continue in a new generation to come (Num. 14:20–24). Later, when the people rebel and are plagued by poisonous snakes, the intercession of Moses leads to the instruction from God to construct a bronze snake as a way of escape (Num. 21:4–9). This immediate deliverance is so powerful a demonstration of God's provision that Jesus applies it as pointing to his own death on the cross (John 3:14). In both cases the saving faith is not towards the visible logic of the event so much as in taking God's promise at face value. The final recorded words of Moses are not directly a prayer, but a proclamation of the deeds of the Lord. However, as we will see from some of the Psalms, a major way of praising God in Israel is to do it in this indirect way, by words addressed to the people telling them of the marvellous doings of God in creation and redemption (Deut. 32:1–43; 33:1–29). There would seem to be an overlap between praise addressed to God and praise of God addressed to others.

We conclude this survey of the prayers of Moses by noting that little is said about the prayer of the ordinary Israelite. Prayer is emphasized as the function of the prophet. There is a reason for this. The one who speaks God's word to the people also stands as the mediator of the people's word to God. In our examination of the relationship of prayer to the person of Christ we saw that he is the word of God to people and the word of people to God. Without this mediation, human prayer is impossible and meaningless. The Old Testament narrative thus far has emphasized this perspective by focusing on the prayer of the mediating ministers of God.

Prayer and the judges

Following the definitive and related roles of Moses as prophet and intercessor, the biblical narrative concentrates on some other significant and unique ministries. Joshua succeeds Moses in the leadership of Israel and brings to it a more warrior-like dimension. He, like Moses, is mediator of the fulfilment of the covenant promises. The miraculous crossing of the Jordan to take possession of the land is likened to the escape across the Red Sea (Josh. 3:1–17; 4:19–24). When the disobedience of Achan brings the threat of judgment on the people, Joshua turns to God in distress and prayer (Josh. 7:7–9). After the capture of Jericho and Ai, Joshua leads the people in the worship of God in a manner that emphasizes his Moses-like role (Josh. 8:30–35). But his major task is to take possession of the land and to apportion it among the tribes of Israel. In this way the covenant promises of God reached a fulfilment that anticipates the glory of a future kingdom under David and Solomon.

Under the judges the process continues. The people rebel, suffer judgment, cry out for deliverance and are saved by a Spirit-anointed judge raised up by God. One such judge is Deborah who, after a significant victory against the Canaanites, sings a psalm of praise that is clearly based on the covenant promises (Judg. 5:1–31). The prayers of the judges reflect their position as chosen deliverers of Israel (Judg. 6:36–40). However, the prayer of Gideon and his testing of God with the fleece needs to be carefully understood. Many Christians have taken this 'putting out of the fleece' as justifying their demanding of God a particular sign to assure them that their decision in a particular matter is the right one. The fact that Gideon seems arbitrarily to choose the sign is seen to justify our choosing anything as a sign. What is overlooked is that Gideon's prayer acknowledges that he is skating on very thin ice and provoking the Lord to anger (Judg. 6:36–40). The point is that his prayer and his fleece-test are misplaced.[11] Gideon has been called for this task and assured that God the mighty warrior is with him. He has been told that he will deliver Israel from the Midianites and God, in condescending mercy, has already given him a sign (Judg. 6:11–24). That should have been more than enough, yet he still demands another sign. But God is merciful and grants it. The use of this narrative to justify such an approach to guidance is clearly misplaced, and ignores an enormous amount of biblical material on guidance. Although Gideon gains confidence and routs the Midianites, he is weak and vacillating and eventually falls into idolatry (Judg. 8:22–28).

Samson the judge, also weak, unwise and easily ensnared, is still used by God to break the hold of the Philistines over Israel. His final prayer is that God will strengthen him so that he can wreak vengeance on the Philistines. Thus among the judges there is the continuing pattern of prayer that we saw established with the patriarchs and particularly with Moses. Little or nothing is said of the ordinary Israelite's understanding of and recourse to prayer. The emphasis remains on the prayer of the covenant functionaries, and on the focus of their prayers towards the fulfilment of the covenant promises. Prayers of thanksgiving and praise are usually in response to the perceived faithfulness of God to his covenant or his steadfast love (*ḥeseḏ*).

---

11. This is a classic example of a biblical event taken over by evangelical piety without due examination of the real situation being reported. There is not the slightest encouragement for us to 'put out a fleece' in this story of Gideon's vacillating obedience and faith.

Prayer and the temple

Prayer in relation to the temple is a theme that receives prominence as we come to the narratives of the books of Samuel and Kings. Hannah, the childless wife of Elkanah, is no ordinary Israelite, though she doesn't know that at first. She bewails her barrenness and gives herself to prayer at the sanctuary at Shiloh. She vows to give any male child she bears to the service of God as a Nazirite (1 Sam. 1:10–11).[12] This would be a very great sacrifice since it would effectively remove the child from normal family life. The narrative makes it clear that this is all in the plan and purpose of God, and when Hannah gives birth to a male child she fulfils her vow and Samuel, when weaned, is taken to the temple. Then follows Hannah's extraordinary prayer of praise and thanksgiving (1 Sam. 2:1–10). We cannot know whether she is drawing on established hymns or composes her own. Whichever it is, it is truly inspired. It is noteworthy for the implied significance of the event. She exults in the victory given to her by God and goes on to praise God for events far beyond the birth of Samuel. The song ends with the amazing lines:

> The adversaries of the LORD shall be broken to pieces;
>   against them he will thunder in heaven.
> The LORD will judge the ends of the earth;
>   he will give strength to his king
>   and exalt the power of his anointed.
>
> (1 Sam. 2:10)

Even given the morale-boost the birth of Samuel must have been to his formerly tormented mother, this hymn seems a bit over the top as a response to the boy's arrival. The first thing to note is that barrenness would be understood as a failure of the covenant for Hannah. Secondly, the failure of the covenant at one point would signify a failure at all points. Thirdly, the reference to the king and the anointed one is not totally absurd since God had promised such even

---

12. The Nazirite vow is related in Num. 6.

to Abraham. It is the link that Hannah is able to make that is extraordinary. The utterance of a similar kind of hymn by Mary at the angelic annunciation indicates the theological link between the two (Luke 1:46–55).[13] Samuel is destined to be a prophet who foreshadows the role of the anointed King to come, and his birth indicates that God is faithful to his promises to redeem his people.

Thus, Hannah's prayer at the sanctuary is significant. It is a prayer that heralds the raising up of the next great prophet after Moses, who will also fulfil priestly and kingly roles as Moses had done. Samuel's first prayer is in response to the calling of the Lord in the temple. He answers that he is listening! The task he is given is a difficult one, for he must tell his master, Eli, that his household is under judgment. The prayer ministry of the adult Samuel, also like that of Moses, is principally seen as intercession on behalf of a wayward people (1 Sam. 7:8–9). When faced with the tricky question of the people's desire for a king, Samuel turns to the Lord in prayer (1 Sam. 8:6–22). The answer that he receives sets out the nature of the request and where it will lead. Thus, when Saul is appointed king, Samuel withdraws from direct leadership but maintains the role which prophets will continue to have in relation to the kings. He in no way abdicates, as some have interpreted his speech in 1 Samuel 12. Rather he is perceived to be the intercessor and the prophetic conscience of king and people (1 Sam. 12:16–25). And so it is that very soon he must confront Saul about his disobedience and pronounce that his kingship will be taken from him.

David is soon revealed to be Saul's successor, though not until much later, when Saul eventually dies in battle, can he take the kingship. In the meantime he is hunted and rejected. It is not necessary for this survey to try to take on board every example of prayer in the Old Testament. We need only to try to understand the main emphases that are there. Up to this point it is clear that the focus is on the prayers of the major players in the saving history of God's people. These are the leaders who have special functions in mediating the word and will of God to the people. Thus when we come to the

---

13. There seems little doubt that Mary's *Magnificat* deliberately recalls Hannah's song.

kingship, we find the emphasis on the prayers of the kings, and these are again linked with the revealed pattern of redemption and the kingdom of God.

David's prayer in 2 Samuel 7 links covenant and temple together with the function of the king and the function of the son of David as son of God.[14] When this son, Solomon, builds the temple he dedicates it with sacrifice and prayer. Prior to this, and in response to a word from God, Solomon prays for wisdom to rule his people well (1 Kgs. 3:5–10). The way the story of Solomon is told indicates that his positive achievements in the kingdom, including the building of the temple, are all linked with his wisdom. In addition, his wisdom flourishes in the context of the climax of God's revelation of the nature of redemption and the kingdom.[15] The significant thing about Solomon's prayer of dedication, the longest prayer recorded up to this point in the Old Testament, is the conjunction of prayer, wisdom, kingship as a covenant office and the temple (1 Kgs. 8:22–53). The temple was for Israel the focal point of all God's dealings with them. It was the visible indication of his presence with them and of his faithfulness to his covenant promises. In other words, the temple, and all it stood for, was what made sense of the universe. Thus Solomon's prayer reiterates the theme of people turning to God and praying in or towards 'this house'. This includes the humbling of the people and repentance of their wicked ways so that reconciliation and restoration can take place at the temple (2 Chr. 7:12–16).

Solomon's prayer gives us some important pointers to the matters we discussed at the outset in relation to prayer and the Trinity. First, the basis of Solomon's prayer is the covenant promises to David and God's faithfulness to these (1 Kgs. 8:23–24). Second, the source of the prayer is the word of God, so that Solomon mainly prays that God

---

14. This has been discussed in chapter 4 and need not be repeated here.

15. I have dealt with this aspect of Solomon's wisdom in greater detail in *Gospel and Wisdom: Israel's Wisdom Literature in the Christian Life*, now reprinted in *The Goldsworthy Trilogy* (Carlisle: Paternoster, 2000); see also my book, *The Tree of Life: Reading Proverbs Today* (Sydney: AIO, 1993), and 'Proverbs' in *New Dictionary of Biblical Theology* (Leicester: Inter-Varsity Press; Downers Grove: InterVarsity Press, 2000).

will do what he has promised (vv. 25–26). We note also that Solomon recognizes that, though God makes his name to dwell in the temple, his real dwelling is in heaven. The temple, then, is the gateway to heaven and to the true throne of God (vv. 27–30). The rest of the prayer (vv. 31–53) enumerates various situations when it is appropriate for people to avail themselves of this access to God. Each one of them involves the vindication of God's name (his character), his grace, and his promises of redemption. All these elements point towards and foreshadow Jesus as the kingly son of David, the true wisdom of God, the true temple and the gateway to God's throne in heaven. Thus here, as in the New Testament, we see that prayer is towards the gospel and its fulfilment. Solomon in effect prays, 'Your kingdom come'. It is significant that Solomon exercises the combined ministry of prophet (1 Kgs. 8: 56, 61), priest (vv. 57–60, 62–64), king and wise man in his dedication of the temple. As to the latter, the building of the temple and the dedicatory prayer stand as the high point of Solomon's exercise of his gift of wisdom from God (1 Kgs. 3:5–14; 4:29–34).[16]

The biblical narrative continues to refer to prayers made by prophets or kings.[17] The prayers of Elijah and Elisha are made in the context of their miracles (1 Kgs. 17:20–22; 18:36–37; 2 Kgs. 4:33; 6:17–18).[18] Elijah's contest with the prophets of Baal on Mount Carmel is more than a demonstration of Yahweh's triumph over non-gods. Elijah rebuilds the altar of the Lord according to his word in the Law. At the appointed time he offers the burnt offering for sin,

---

16. The whole passage of 1 Kgs. 3–10 focuses on Solomon's wisdom. The temple is the greatest expression of this wisdom, while Solomon's wisdom-conquest of the Queen of Sheba (1 Kgs. 10) points to the incoming of the Gentiles to the temple.

17. James tells us that Elijah prayed for there to be no rain (Jas. 5:17–18). The narrative in the book of Kings does not mention prayer but only Elijah's prophetic pronouncement (1 Kgs. 17:1; 18:1, 41).

18. There are three main clusters of miracles in the Bible: the redemption from Egypt under Moses; the ministry of Elijah and Elisha; and the gospel event and its immediate sequel in Acts. These clearly have significance as focal points in the revelation of salvation.

and prays that Yahweh will demonstrate that he is God in Israel. It is a call to Israel to return to the covenant relationship with God, to believe the gospel as it is foreshadowed in the Old Testament.

The confession of sin

In the historical narratives of the Old Testament there is one other type of prayer that becomes quite significant when the fortunes of Israel are clouded by disaster, particularly when the nation suffers exile and alienation from the promised land: the acknowledgment of the propensity of the people to break the covenant. In the midst of the tumult of the empire changing hands from the Babylonians to the Persians, Daniel is moved by the prophecy of Jeremiah concerning their exile. He turns to prayer, confessing the sins of his people and acknowledging that the calamity that has befallen them is their own fault (Dan. 9:1–19). The heart of the prayer is Daniel's recalling of the redemptive experience of the exodus from Egypt, and the prayer that God would be merciful to forgive and to restore the desolated sanctuary in Jerusalem. He recognizes that the longed-for salvation of Israel will restore the glory of the name of Yahweh that the nation bears.

In the post-exilic community, Ezra turns in embarrassed prayer to God, confessing the sins of the returned exiles who have quickly turned to covenant-breaking behaviour (Ezra 9:5–15). In this case many of the people join with him and there are concerted moves to deal with the particular sin of mixed marriages. Nehemiah, still in exile in Persia, hears of the misfortune that has befallen those already returned to the land. He confesses the sins of the people and pleads their cause on the grounds of the covenant (Neh. 1:4–11). Later, in company with the Levites, Ezra prays at length (Neh. 9:6–37). In great detail he rehearses the redemptive history of Israel, beginning with the creation, the calling of Abraham and the exodus. The basis of his appeal to the Lord, then, is the covenant faithfulness of God in the past (vv. 32–33). He retells the story of redemption, and recalls the saving acts of God for them. The outcome is a covenant renewal and many reforms according to the revealed will of God. In the Old Testament, as in the New, what moves us to prayer and the expression of true repentance and faithful commitment to God is the gospel, the declaration of what great things God has done for us in his Son, Jesus Christ.

Salvation history and the knowledge of God

The God to whom we pray is the creator of heaven and earth. He is the sustainer of all things by the word of his power. This ongoing providential action of God in the world is what makes up everything that we include under the idea of history. Therefore, we can assert that all world history is directly or indirectly the history of God's covenant. In this realm of history God has been pleased to reveal himself so that we can know him. The universe, natural history, and the affairs of the nations of the world are all eloquent of God's being and providential care. This is the knowledge of God that sinful humanity suppresses in its wickedness (Rom. 1:18). The covenantal revelation of God is the gracious way God overcomes this sinful suppression. Through the covenant of salvation he calls us to himself that we might know him and relate to him as he intended. The stark contrasts between the blatant forms of idolatry and the true knowledge of God that emerge in Old Testament history are instructive. It is too superficial to see the differences between what invites God's approbation and what provokes his judgment as a matter of the levels of ethical sophistication. Nor can we write them off merely in terms of polytheism versus monotheism. The knowledge of God is too carefully defined by his covenant word and actions. Many forms of idolatry arise that are subtler than the polytheistic worship of Israel's neighbours, and are even warned against in the New Testament. Anything that substitutes for the knowledge of God as he reveals himself is idolatry.

It perhaps needs to be said that knowledge of the God of the covenant can be quite minimal for some Christians. The covenant implications of the basics of the gospel may be little understood by a new convert, but it must never be said that such a newcomer has no true knowledge of God. To grasp the basic truth, 'Jesus died for my sins and I trust him for salvation,' is to grasp, without realizing it, the central truth of the covenant. The death and resurrection of Jesus fulfil the covenant promises and, thus, reveal the God of the covenant. But to remain at such a basic level without a growth in understanding, to deny oneself the richness of the revelation of the covenant in the Old Testament as well as in the New, is to stunt our knowledge of God and to deny ourselves the spiritual health of wisdom and assurance. Such a state of affairs will inevitably stifle prayer, leaving it undernourished and vulnerable. Above all, in this part of the Old Testament under consideration, we see the way prayer is a response to the covenant commitment of a gracious God. Even in the face of human failure, he is faithful and shows mercy to those who seek him and call upon his name.

Summary

- Prayer in the New Testament is presented as the climax and fulfilment of prayer in the Old Testament.
- Biblical theology surveys the history of God's people and notes that God must first address his people before they can have anything to say to him.
- Prayer is tied to the covenant-relationship of the people to God, who know God only through this relationship.
- The Old Testament emphasizes the function of the mediators of the covenant – prophets, priests, judges and kings – as intercessors for the people.
- The high point of Israel's history comes with Solomon, who links prayer with kingship, wisdom, covenant and temple.

Pause a moment . . .

When you think about your relationship with God as a praying person, do you think mainly about:

- your practice of approaching God in prayer, or
- your mediator who makes prayer possible through his intercession for you?

Take some time to reflect on the Old Testament emphasis on the covenant functionaries (prophets, priests and kings) as those whose role it is to pray for the people. Then consider how these roles point forward to, and are fulfilled in, the person and work of Jesus Christ.

The progress of prayer
8 II. The Psalms

The Psalms in the scheme of the Old Testament

The book of Psalms belongs in the context of Israel's history as an ongoing expression of faith. It deserves separate treatment since it is made up of mostly hymns of praise to God and various other kinds of prayers. A few individual psalms are crafted as instruction or wisdom poetry. These are not addressed directly to God, but to the people of God, or they reflect on the psalmist's experience of God and his salvation. It is now thought that the whole collection of psalms as we have it in the Bible was assembled in the period after the exile with the overall purpose of instruction.[1] At the same time the individual psalms model the nature of prayer in the life of Israel. Titles to individual psalms indicate that the collection is largely pre-exilic, the

1. The exile of the people of Judah into Babylon began with two major deportations in 597 and 586 BC. The Persian emperor Cyrus, through his edict of return in 538, permitted the return of the Jews to their homeland. Psalm 137 reflects on the experience in Babylon and thus indicates a post-exilic date for the formation of the collection as we now have it in the book of Psalms.

largest number being assigned to David and one to Moses. The Hebrew name given to the book is *tᵉhillîm*, which means praises.[2]

There has been a great deal of discussion in scholarly circles about where the Psalms fit into the scheme of things in the Old Testament. Liberal scholars were generally more concerned to understand the historical origins of the individual compositions but applied a whole series of presuppositions that robbed their interpretation of any real spiritual value. Then interest began to focus on the forms that the various psalms took, and on what might be deduced from the characteristics of the circumstances under which they were written. Conservative scholars felt that the tradition of assigning the bulk of the psalms to King David needed to be preserved in the face of critical scepticism about the titles of the individual psalms, and especially those linking them with David. By maintaining the position that the psalms were mostly written by David it was felt that this assisted in linking the individual psalms to Jesus, the messianic successor to David. But in so doing, the titles ascribing certain psalms to other authors tended to be overlooked. It is worth remembering that the titles are a part of the Hebrew text and not a small-print appendage as they appear in our English versions.[3] The titles must be accorded the same authority as any other part of the biblical text.

While taking seriously the Davidic titles, it is not necessary to assign every psalm to David in order to see its relationship to, and fulfilment in, the ministry of Christ. If we consider the Christology of the New Testament, we see that Jesus is proclaimed as fulfilling all the possible roles of Old Testament people, including that of the ordinary Israelite. The supreme paradox is that even the evildoers and the ungodly have their fulfilment in Christ. We see this in the way the seriousness of human evil and rejection of God bring the

---

2. This word comes from the same Hebrew verb root (*hll*) as the word *hallᵉlû*, the imperative form that is usually joined to the shortened form of the name of God, *Jah*. Thus, *hallelujah* means 'praise God' (plural imperative).
3. Thus, in Hebrew Bibles the title is usually all or part of verse 1, which has the effect of making the verse numbering different from that in English Bibles. The Hebrew text is indeed translated faithfully, but it is printed in a form that suggest that the titles are not part of the original psalms.

manifestation of God's judgment at the cross of Calvary. In being made sin for us (2 Cor. 5:21), Jesus takes our place by accepting the role of evildoer for us, and defines the true nature of sin and the wrath of God upon it. There is, therefore, no aspect of the Psalms in the Old Testament that does not point to Jesus and find its ultimate meaning in him.[4] We are principally concerned here with the nature of prayer as it is revealed in the Psalms. Up to this point, our survey has shown that the main emphasis in the Old Testament historical narratives is on the prayers of certain significant figures whose function in Israel clearly foreshadows the messianic ministry of Jesus. This fact alone highlights the connection between prayer and the ministry of Jesus. It also shows the covenant context of prayer. The covenant is first and foremost a unilateral relationship based on promises that God graciously establishes with his people. By unilateral we mean that God did not hold discussions with Abraham, or seek human permission or insights on the matter, but simply did it according to his own will. This points to the fact of the initiation of prayer by God through his self-revelation.

Once we establish the link between prayer in the Old Testament and the messianic function of Jesus, we are able to observe the nature of the prayers in the book of Psalms to see how they help us to understand this link. An examination of the types of prayer in the Psalms should provide some insights as to why the New Testament proceeds in the direction it does in its teaching about prayer.

How the Christian connects with the Psalms

As we have seen, Jesus fulfils the role of ordinary human being as well as fulfilling the special ministry roles in the Old Testament. We should have no difficulty in recognizing the main covenant functionaries

---

4. Bruce Waltke, 'A Canonical Process Approach to the Psalms', in J. Feinberg and P. Feinberg (eds.), *Traditions and Testament* (Chicago: Moody Press, 1981), maintains that the Psalms are 'ultimately the prayers of Jesus Christ, son of God. He alone is worthy to pray the ideal vision of a king suffering for righteousness and emerging victorious over the hosts of evil.'

whose ministries are brought to a climactic fulfilment in the ministry of Jesus. The Christology of historic Christianity involves the recognition of the way Jesus is proclaimed as the goal of these ministries. His roles as prophet, priest and king are the most obvious in this regard. To these I would want to add his being the wise man or sage. Thus the Sermon on the Mount, in which Matthew's version of the Lord's Prayer is given, concludes with a classic wisdom saying contrasting wisdom and foolishness (Matt. 7: 24–29). This suggests that the Lord's Prayer is presented in the Sermon on the Mount as part of Jesus' definitive wisdom. The authority with which he spoke, and which marked him out from the wise teachers of Israel, indicates that he is perceived to be the source of true wisdom. God's wisdom, so often associated with his creation of an orderly universe, is now given its greatest expression in the person and work of Jesus by which the creation is being renewed. We have also seen how the prophet played the part of the intercessor, a function also exercised by the king on occasions. We may assume that some form of prayer accompanied the priestly ministries, especially those involving the offering of sacrifice and of incense.[5]

But what do we make of the prayer of the ordinary Israelite? Leaving aside the question of the titles of the individual psalms and the authorship they claim, there is every indication that the whole collection was taken over quite early as public property. The book of Psalms thus represents a new emphasis over that of the historical narratives that focused on prayer as mediated by the prophet, priest or king. Many scholars have accepted it as functioning as the hymnbook of the second temple in the post-exilic nation. There are at least two guides to answering the question of how the Christian connects with the Psalms. The first is the way the various functionaries, whose roles are fulfilled in the ministry of Jesus, represented the ordinary people. The second is the way the ordinary people were also fulfilled in Jesus.

---

5. Although the significance of incense is not specifically named in the relevant texts, it was offered along with the sacrificial offerings. The high priest burned incense in the sanctuary so that the cloud would cover the mercy seat (Lev. 16:13). Ps. 141:2 links prayer with incense, a connection also found in Rev. 5:8; 8:3–4.

Jesus is not only the Son of Abraham and the Son of David; he is also the Son of Adam.[6] The prophets represented the people in receiving the word of God; the priests represented them in sacrificing to God and in being able to stand in the presence of God in the sanctuary; and the kings represented the whole of the covenant nation as the sons of God. When we come to the New Testament we see how the various authors present Jesus as the true prophet, our great high priest, and the kingly son of David. But he is also presented as the true Israel and as the faithful Adam. When a psalm lacks clear identification as the work of David, this in no way weakens its testimony to the role Jesus was to play on our behalf as the true and faithful human covenant partner of God. Kingship is clearly not the only Old Testament role that Jesus fulfils.

You may ask why I am so concerned to establish this link with Jesus. Is it not true that we can identify with the psalm writers simply on the basis of our being, as they were, children of the God and Father of our Lord Jesus Christ, who is also the God of Abraham, Isaac and Jacob? This is indeed true, and many of the psalms can be read and applied as they stand by the Christian believer without any great effort of interpretation. It is true provided that, and this is a big proviso, we recognize that our only way to the God of the psalmist is through the mediation of Jesus Christ. As Christians we must never allow ourselves for one moment to think that we have another direct line to God in heaven. 'There is one God, and there is one mediator between God and men, the man Christ Jesus.' If we ignore this saying of Paul in 1 Timothy 2:5 we are in danger of leaving Christ out of the equation. A moment's reflection should convince us that when we, as Christians, read a psalm that seems to invite us to identify more or less directly with the psalmist, we are assuming that his God is Jesus' Father, whom we know only through the Son. If this does not convince you, reflect again on those psalms in which the writer speaks overtly as an Israelite, refers to the temple in Jerusalem, or refers to his ancestors who came out of Egypt in the exodus. We can be spared the problem of deciding which psalms we can identify with and which ones we must engage in some kind of interpretative

6. As we are reminded by the genealogy of Luke 3.

shift. All we need to do is to apply a consistent principle of Old Testament interpretation and we will find that all the psalms, without exception, point us to the person and work of Jesus. Thus, as a consequence of this reference to Christ, they point to us who are 'in Christ' and who are thus defined by who Jesus is. This Jesus is not an unapproachable deity, but is the true God-Man whose humanity expresses that which our humanity is being redeemed to become.

It should be evident, then, that when the psalmist speaks of coming before God in his holy sanctuary in Jerusalem, or going into the house of the Lord, we cannot read this as referring to our going into a church building. If the temple was the centre and focal point of the holy city Jerusalem, and if Jerusalem as the holy city of David was the focal point of the promised land, and if it was at this temple that fellowship with God was expressed and maintained through the sacrificial ministry, we may well ask how such things relate to us. The answer is, of course, that Jesus is identified as transferring all these things to himself. He is the new temple, the place where God and his people meet and are reconciled. It is clear from John 2:19–22 and Acts 13:32–33 that the restored temple promised by the prophets is the resurrection body of Jesus. That is why, as Jesus proclaimed to the Samaritan woman in John 4:21–23, there is no longer a holy city or holy land on earth. The only temple we can go to now is the temple where Jesus is. The fact that Jesus is absent from us speaks of the temple that is in heaven (Heb. 8:1–7; 9:11–12). The fact that he is also present with us by his Spirit speaks of the household of God, the body of Christ, the temple of the Holy Spirit (Eph. 2:19–21; 1 Pet. 2:1–10). The temple is both at the same time the temple in heaven and the gathering of the believers here on earth that the Spirit of Christ indwells. Despite common Christian practice to refer to part or all of a church building as the sanctuary, this is very misleading and tends to detract from the biblical reality.[7]

7. In the same way, Christian tour operators who advertise trips to the 'Holy Land' are promising something that it is not in their power to give. By all means let us visit the lands of the Bible to learn something of their geography and history, but to make pilgrimages to them as 'Holy' is to confuse the biblical evidence and is little different from the veneration of other kinds of 'holy relics'.

Types of prayer in the Psalms

It is not necessary for us to make a detailed examination of the psalms. It is enough that we try to understand what kind of prayers they represent. Scholars who engage in what is known as form criticism have drawn attention to the fact that we can classify various forms; however, despite the term *form*, this is more often than not a classification based on content analysis.[8] Unfortunately these critics frequently applied unbiblical presuppositions in their analysis and consequently drew unsustainable conclusions about the place and function of the psalms in Israel's worship. There is, however, no reason why we should not take a leaf out of their book by applying a simple procedure of classification in order to see what different facets of prayer were understood and used.

The question of who wrote an individual psalm may sometimes help us determine something of the original significance of what is said. In the final analysis, however, the application to us as Christians must be through the common link that all the different kinds of authors have with Christ the fulfiller. Since many of the psalms involve more that one form and theme, for example when complaint and prayer for deliverance give way to praise for deliverance, I will concentrate on the main themes to be found. Even though our familiarity with the book of Psalms means that there will be few surprises, it will be informative to isolate some of the main themes and to reflect on their significance.

---

8. A pioneer of this method was the German scholar, Hermann Gunkel, who identified the following major classifications: Hymns; Communal Laments; Royal Psalms; Individual Laments; and Individual Songs of Thanksgiving. For examples of the way these classifications have been employed, see R. J. V. Hiebert, 'Psalms, Theology of', in Walter Elwell (ed.), *Evangelical Dictionary of Biblical Theology* (Grand Rapids: Baker; Carlisle: Paternoster, 1996); and Leopold Sabourin, *The Psalms: Their Origin and Meaning* (New York: Alba House, 1974). A useful evangelical treatment is Geoffrey W. Grogan, *Prayer, Praise and Prophecy: A Theology of the Psalms* (Fearn: Mentor, 2001). See also Grogan's article, 'Psalms', in *New Dictionary of Biblical Theology* (Leicester: Inter-Varsity Press; Downers Grove: InterVarsity Press, 2000).

As I mentioned in chapter 1, it is sometimes suggested that prayer is a word properly applied only to requests. There is some basis for this in the way the various words are used in the Bible.[9] The ground that we have covered thus far would support the view that the common English usage to cover a range of types of address is valid. I would rather speak of different kinds of prayer.[10] A number of different types of prayer may be identified in the Psalms.[11]

Prayers of complaint about suffering, false accusations or persecution[12]

We have little difficulty in identifying with these, particularly as the specific form of suffering or persecution is not usually indicated. Sometimes there is the cry of longing, such as, 'How long, O Lord?' These prayers are similar to those expressing the sense of being forsaken by God.[13] The psalmists here give expression to the common lot of the people of God, since to be aligned with God is to be at enmity with a world that rejects him and hates his claim to be sovereign Lord over it.

---

9. *Theological Dictionary of the New Testament* (Grand Rapids: Eerdmans, 1964), Vol. 2, pp. 775–808.
10. It is true that the word prayer in the Psalms is used exclusively of petition. We should not be hung up on word usage, however, as we are concerned with the broader reality of speaking to God. The book of Psalms, along with the rest of the biblical evidence, supports the notion of several different types of address that we may refer to as prayer.
11. Within the individual psalms more than one type of prayer will often be found, which is not surprising given the link all prayer has to the words and actions of God.
12. Such prayers are contained in, for example, Pss. 5; 7; 10; 17; 22; 26, and many others.
13. Cries to the Lord of 'How long?' are found in Pss. 6:3; 13:1–2; 35:17; 74:9–10; 94:3; 119:84. Some of these express the sense of abandonment to God's anger; others are more directly concerned with persecution.

Prayer expressing the sense of being forsaken by God, but sometimes followed by words of confidence[14]

This theme is closely linked with the complaints, but is a more extreme form of it. Perhaps the most desperate sounding cry is the one Jesus took to himself on the cross: 'My God, my God, why have you forsaken me?' This use of Psalm 22 is instructive. There is no reason to believe that this terrible cry of desolation means that Jesus had lost all faith. The mystery of Jesus' forsakenness must ever remain part of the glory of the cross. That Jesus underwent, for our sake, this terrible break in his fellowship with his Father is our guarantee that we, however forsaken we feel, are never out of the Father's care. Jesus knew the outcome would be his resurrection.[15] In the psalm itself the cry and the following complaint about the persecutors give way to the most extraordinary words of confidence and praise for deliverance. So remarkable is this transition that some scholars have suggested that the psalm reflected the complaint made before a priest at the temple. The priest then, on the basis of the covenant, gave a reassurance of salvation that evoked the praise.[16]

Prayer for deliverance from suffering or one's enemies[17]

This is one of the most frequently occurring themes in the book of Psalms. It expresses the distress of either the individual psalmist or of the whole people of God. This, and the two themes mentioned above, take a realistic view of the world in which we live. Again there is a clear sense of the suffering that comes from being aligned with the God of heaven. We may include here those prayers for the righteous judgment of God upon the enemies and persecutors of the

---

14. See Pss. 6; 13; 22; 38.

15. Matt. 17:9, 22–23; 20:18–19; Mark 9:9, 31; John 10:18; 12:23, 34.

16. Form critics have suggested that the priestly assurance might well have been in the form of an oracle of salvation beginning with the familiar phrase 'Fear not'. The supporting evidence for this is the way the phrase is used, for example, in Isaiah to introduce assurances of salvation (Is. 35:4; 40:9; 41:10, 13, 14; 43:1, 5). Though, if this is the case, why the assurance of salvation is not stated in the psalm is not clear.

17. For example, Pss. 3; 6; 7; 17; 22; 31; 43; 59; 70; 71; 120; 129:5–6; 137:7–9.

godly. Thus, as in the book of Proverbs, there is a frequent comparison of the righteous status of the believer with that of the godless persecutors. We do not have to look far in the New Testament to see that this dynamic of the spiritual life has not changed.

Prayer extolling God's **ḥeseḏ**[18] *or covenant faithfulness and compassion*[19]

This is an indispensable theme in the book of Psalms that we must understand if we are to avoid misuse of the sense of assurance that is evident in so many psalms. The confidence that the penitent and complaining people of God express is not a groundless optimism. From time to time we meet people who claim to have made their peace with God. It is worth probing to see whether this optimism is properly grounded in what God says. Has God made peace with them on the basis of the atoning work of Christ, or are they saying that they no longer fear God? Praying when the mood takes us does not make peace with God. Nor does the conviction that we are essentially decent people. Peace with God is firmly grounded on the work of Christ and on that alone. He is the fulfilment of all the covenant promises that the psalmists refer to when recalling God's *ḥeseḏ*, his covenant love and compassion. All the references in the Psalms to the mighty acts of God, his covenant and his steadfast love point us to the new covenant in Christ, and to his mighty acts to redeem us.

---

18. The Hebrew word *ḥeseḏ* occurs some 130 times in the Psalms. In the NRSV and ESV it is usually translated as 'steadfast love'. In the Old Testament as a whole it is a word used of both God and people. However, in Psalms its subject is almost exclusively God: it is God's *ḥeseḏ* that gives the psalmist confidence in praying to him. It speaks of God's faithfulness to his purposes of grace, especially as expressed in the covenant with Israel, to act consistently, justly and mercifully towards his people.
19. For example, Pss. 5:7; 13:5; 18:50; 25:6, 10; 33:5, 18, 22; 36:7, 10; 40:11; 42:8; 44:26; 59:17; 69:16; 89:1, 2, 14, 24, 28, 33, 49; 103:17; 106:1, 7, 45; 107:1, 8, 15, 21, 31, 43. Note the praise refrain in every verse of Ps. 136.

Prayer of the king, or prayer acknowledging the Davidic king-messiah[20]

Jesus' messianic pedigree involves both his divine and eternal nature as God the Son, and his human descent from King David. The latter is often stressed in the New Testament because of the miracle of God becoming a man, and because it was only as man that he could save our humanity. It is important to the New Testament writers because it linked Jesus of Nazareth with the whole structure of Israel's history as the people of God. Jesus did not come to obliterate the Old Testament hope, but to fulfil it and to make clear its full glory. Christians can identify with the prayers of David because they point to the mediatorial role of Jesus. Peter concludes his Pentecost sermon with the declaration that, 'God has made him both Lord and Christ [Messiah], this Jesus whom you crucified' (Acts 2:36). Once again Christology, and particularly the function of Christ as mediator, is the very heart of Christian prayer.

Prayer expressing trust and confidence in God[21]

This kind of prayer is often linked with complaint about suffering. The confidence that God will answer the petition for relief hangs together with the confidence in God's covenant promises. It points us to the fact that faith is nothing less than taking God at his word and having complete confidence that he will not, and cannot, deceive us. In our discussion on prayer and faith in chapter 5 we considered the nature of faith as defined by its object. So often in the Psalms the writer expresses confidence in God, or is reminded of the grounds of confidence, because of the way God has dealt with Israel in his great saving acts in the past. In the same way the mighty deeds of God in sending Jesus to live and die for us, and in raising him from the dead, fill us with confidence that he remains true to his promises. The prayer of faith is one that takes the promises of God at face value, not one that holds God to things he has not promised.

---

20. Pss. 2; 18; 21; 45; 72; 89; 110; 132.

21. Pss. 6; 7; 13; 22; 23; 28; 54; 56; 71; 109; 140.

Prayer praising God for who and what he is, and for his marvellous deeds[22]

The psalms of praise are particularly instructive in that they show us that the praise of God is not merely an expression of awe before some indescribable greatness. Rather they take the form of recounting the deeds of God in creation and salvation. To tell what God has done in the redemption of his people is at the heart of praise. Sometimes this is made very personal when the psalm tells of how God has dealt with the individual psalmist. But these individual expressions of deliverance are always within the wider context of the covenant people. Thus the more significant expressions of praise are those that recount something of the covenant history of the people, and specifically the national experience of redemption.

Prayer involving recital of the history of salvation[23]

These recitals are a specific form of praise of God for his redemptive acts. What makes them so significant is that they focus on the Old Testament's foreshadowing of the objective gospel. In the New Testament the witness of Christians is applied primarily to the relating of what God has done for his people in the person and work of Jesus Christ. There is nothing wrong in praising God for what he has done in us, but this should never replace the major biblical emphasis on what God has done for us.

Prayer invoking, or rejoicing in, the judgment of God[24]

I noted in the discussion of the Lord's Prayer that the petition for the coming of the kingdom reminds us that this kingdom will not be consummated without the final, terrible judgment of God. It the Old Testament this significant connection between salvation and judgment is everywhere in evidence. It begins with the word of grace

22. Pss. 9; 26; 40; 44; 65; 66; 71; 73; 75; 78; 86; 92; 96; 103; 104; 105; 106; 107; 111; 118; 141; 145; 150.

23. Pss. 78; 105; 106; 114; 136. Ps. 68 also contains many references to God's saving acts for Israel.

24. Pss. 7; 9; 36; 50; 58; 67; 94; 96; 98; 137; 149. Notice how frequently judgment is associated with the salvation of God's people.

that accompanies the judgment on Adam and Eve. The salvation of Noah and his family occurs in the midst of judgment on the whole world. Israel's salvation from slavery in Egypt is inseparable from the judgment upon the Egyptians. In fact, we have to recognize that salvation is an act of God's judgment. This explains something of what lies behind the prayers for judgment on Israel's enemies. Sometimes these seem to be vindictive, and have evoked a sense of moral outrage in some people. Of course it is possible for even God's people to allow the baser feelings of revenge to rise within them, but that does not change the fact that no redemption in the Bible occurs without judgment. Nor can we write off the imprecations of some psalms as merely the baser emotions coming out. Thus for example, Psalms 96 and 98 conclude with a general call to rejoice because 'he comes to judge the earth'. The final proof of this redemption-judgment nexus is seen on the cross of Jesus as he saves us by bearing the full weight of God's wrath on sin. It also accounts for the apparent preoccupation of the book of Revelation with final judgment as the necessary precursor to the consummation of the kingdom.

The significance of the Psalms for prayer

For any Christian for whom prayer is becoming formal and stereotyped, the Psalms provide a rich source of inspiration. It is true that to read the Psalms on your knees, as it were, can be a great boost to one's prayer experience. The book of Psalms provides the most sustained and concentrated biblical expressions of prayer. There are two qualifications I would make to this recommendation to resort directly to the Psalms for prayers. The first is to remember that the Psalms express the believer's responses to the revelation of God when it was yet to be completed with the coming of Jesus. All the details of the individual psalms need to be refracted through their fulfilment in Christ. The Christian needs to develop a sense of the way Israelite functionaries (king, prophet, priest, wise man, ordinary believer), places (Jerusalem, Zion, promised land) and institutions (temple and its ministry, sacrifice, feasts such as Passover) are all given their definitive expression in the person and work of Christ. The same must be said for the frequently referred to acts of God in creation, redemption and judgment. The second qualification is that the Psalms are only one part of the progression of revelation about prayer. We should never isolate the specific forms of expression in the Psalms from prayer as it is revealed in prophetic eschatology,[25] in the person of Jesus, and in the post-resurrection prayers of the Apostles.

The bottom line, then, in considering the contribution of the Psalms to our understanding of the nature of authentic prayer, is that prayer is always prayer towards the fulfilling of God's redemption plan for people and for the whole of creation. All the dimensions of the gospel of Christ are present in Old Testament form, that is, as prefigurements or foreshadowings of that which is given its final expression in Jesus of Nazareth. The gospel will not permit us to view the Psalms in any other way. Some might ask why we need the Old Testament expressions if everything contained in them finds a fuller expression in the New Testament. The answer is that the New Testament presupposes the Old and thus we do not grasp as well as we should the meaning of the New if we sever it from the Old. The Old Testament, in so many ways, gives us the texture of the gospel. It shows us in great detail what it is that Jesus achieves in his death and resurrection. We must read the two Testaments as a unit if we are to avoid an irrational cleavage of understanding of Christian existence into an Old Testament form and a New Testament form.

The Psalms and the knowledge of God

There are a number of individual psalms that refer to knowledge of or about God. While it is true that there is an important distinction between knowing about God and knowing him, it is also true that the biblical evidence is that to know God goes hand in hand with knowing about him. The distinction, in popular evangelical expression, between head knowledge and heart knowledge does have some biblical warrant. But we must remember that the biblical usage of

---

25. Prophetic eschatology, the subject of chapter 9, refers to the view expressed in the prophetic literature about the future coming of God to save his people and bring in his glorious kingdom.

heart, unlike common modern usage, does not primarily mean the emotions. It is rather a reference to the centre of our thinking and will, as well as our affections. In biblical terminology, the heart includes what we designate as the head. For example, Isaiah distinguishes between a merely formal use of words of praise and hearts truly in tune with God:

> (Because) this people draw near with their mouth
>   and honor me with their lips,
> while their hearts are far from me,
> and their fear of me is a commandment taught by men.
>
> (Is. 29:13)

When reverence for God's character and trust in his saving deeds are absent there is no true knowledge of God. On the other hand, as we have seen thus far in our discussion, the knowledge of God is based on a true apprehension of his nature and his deeds as he has revealed them. I would suggest, then, that there is a distinction between knowing about the Lord and knowing the Lord. Yet the latter will always include the former. Thus in the Psalms we find references to knowing that the Lord has done, or will do, something (Pss. 4:3; 20:6; 41:11; 109:27; 140:12), knowing that Yahweh is God (Pss. 46:10; 83:18; 100:3), knowing that God is for the psalmist (Ps. 56:9), knowing the name or ways of the Lord (Pss. 9:10; 25:4; 91:14; 147:20), and knowing God (Pss. 36:10; 87:4). The underlying principle is that God knows his creatures better than they know themselves. To be known by God is the corollary of being made by him. To know ourselves we need the all-knowing God to speak to us.

> O Lord, you have searched me and known me!
> You know when I sit down and when I rise up;
>   you discern my thoughts from afar.
> You search out my path and my lying down
>   and are acquainted with all my ways.
> Even before a word is on my tongue,
>   behold, O Lord, you know it altogether.
> You hem me in, behind and before,
>   and lay your hand upon me.

Such knowledge is too wonderful for me;
  it is high; I cannot attain it.

(Ps. 139:1–6)

The sense of amazement at God's knowledge of us shows that the prayers of the psalmists are reflections of that knowledge.[26] Our investigation into the content of the Psalms also highlighted the prominence of the theme of God's *ḥeseḏ* or steadfast love. This covenant theme provides the grounds for confident prayer. It focuses on the objective fact that our knowledge of God is secondary to and a derivative of God's knowledge of us. For the psalmists, being known by God is being foreknown and chosen to be his people. It is to be the objects of God's saving grace. It is to be given access to the house of the Lord and to his awesome presence. It is to know the assurance of sins forgiven and of ultimate vindication in the face of all enemies. It is to know that God hears the prayers of his faithful people and is pleased with the praises of his flock. Being known by God is the real heart of the book of Psalms, and is the wellspring of prayer.

Summary

- The book of Psalms provides the most extensive examples of prayer and praise as it came to be used by all the people of God in the Old Testament.
- Christians can connect with the individual psalms because all the Old Testament people from whom they came find their fulfilment in Jesus, who is the one mediator between God and us.
- The different kinds of prayer in the Psalms show the different ways prayer came to be used by the people of God.
- The book of Psalms emphasizes the covenant framework for all prayer, and thus foreshadows the person and work of Christ.

---

26. Once again we see illustrated Calvin's argument with which he begins his *Institutes*: to know ourselves we must know God and to know God we must know ourselves.

Pause a moment . . .

If the practice of prayer has become mechanical for you, try beginning your prayer each day by reading a psalm 'on your knees'. As you pray a psalm, think about the pathway from the psalm to you through the mediation of Christ.

Where relevant, reflect on the psalm's testimony to:

- the being and character of God
- the great things he has done for us
- the sufferings we share with the True Israelite, Jesus
- our destiny to 'dwell in the Lord's house forever'
- the fact that God knows us better than we know ourselves.

9 The progress of prayer III. Prophetic eschatology

The prophetic vision of the future kingdom

The historical narrative of the Old Testament comes to a climax with the reign of Solomon and the completion of the temple. This period is clearly the pinnacle of Israel's history because, after Solomon, the kingdom of Israel falls into a decline that leads to eventual destruction. Solomon's wisdom reaches its zenith with this climax of the kingdom and, at the same time, the most detailed and informative expression of prayer occurs in the dedication of the temple. This establishes an important link between the notion of wisdom and prayer. Both are based on the revealed knowledge of God as the framework from within which we interpret our experience of the world. As with wisdom, this association of the kingly prayer of dedication with the temple points to the link between prayer and the kingly reign of Jesus, who is the new temple. This is implied in Peter's Pentecost sermon when he refers to the promises made to David in 2 Samuel 7:14, promises that had their first, but partial, fulfilment in Solomon's reign and the building of the temple. Peter declares that the true fulfilment of these promises takes place in the resurrection of Jesus (Acts 2:30–31). Thus prayer is given its most detailed expression thus far as Solomon's reign centres on the temple in Jerusalem (1 Kgs. 8). Peter understands that the true Davidic king ascends the eternal throne in the resurrection and ascension of Jesus. This would indicate that the prayers of Jesus here on earth, along with his intercession for us in the temple of heaven, fulfil a similar role in the ultimate dedication and sanctification of the new and heavenly temple.

The prophets, whose oracles have been preserved for us in the books bearing their names, each present a picture of the future restoration of a nation under judgment. These so-called writing prophets ministered during the period after the glorious kingdom of David and Solomon had gone into decline. The historical manifestation of the kingdom in fulfilment of the promises to Abraham had turned out to be brittle and transitory. This reversal occurs not because God is unable to fulfil his promises, but because Israel is incorrigible and constantly breaks the covenant. The division of the kingdom after the death of Solomon, the destruction of the northern kingdom of Israel and the Babylonian exile of the people of Judah all occur as judgments upon the faithlessness and covenant-breaking behaviour of the nation. Unlike Israel, God is not faithless, and he shows that his promises are firm. He will not deviate from his purpose to have a redeemed and righteous people who will inherit the promises made to Abraham. The eschatology of the prophets provides a many-faceted view of this kingdom, yet it is one that is coherent and consistent. In essence, the prophets predict the day when God will act in a final and definitive way to save his people and to bring in his kingdom.[1]

It may have seemed that the restoration from Babylon was the point at which the kingdom promises were about to be realized.[2] However, it is quite clear from the narratives of Ezra and Nehemiah,

---

1. I have given a more detailed treatment of the structure of biblical theology in my books *Gospel and Kingdom* (Exeter: Paternoster, 1981); *According to Plan* (Leicester: Inter-Varsity Press, 1991); and *Preaching the Whole Bible as Christian Scripture* (Grand Rapids: Eerdmans; Leicester: Inter-Varsity Press, 2000).
2. Cyrus came to power in 538 BC, after which he issued his edict of return, allowing captive peoples to return home.

and from the post-exilic prophets Haggai, Zechariah and Malachi, that the then restored nation, temple and Jerusalem are but a pale shadow of what is yet to come. Their glory could not even be compared to that which existed before the exile. The Old Testament comes to an end without this kingdom of prophetic eschatology[3] being fulfilled. After a gap of some four hundred years, Jesus of Nazareth begins his ministry and declares that his role is to fulfil all the promises and prophecies of the Old Testament.

The issue of prophetic foretelling is solved by some interpreters by separating prophecies fulfilled in the first coming of Christ from those expected to be fulfilled only in his second coming. It is clear that the New Testament maintains a distinction between the events of the first and second comings of Christ. Whatever we may think about the sequence of events at the end of this age, and whatever we may understand about the fulfilling of prophecy, the New Testament claims that Jesus suffered and died under Pontius Pilate, that he rose and ascended, and that he promised he would come again. However, to distinguish between the two comings of Christ, three if you include his coming by his Spirit at Pentecost, is not the same as saying that some prophecies were fulfilled at his first coming and some have yet to be fulfilled at his second coming.

There is another way of looking at it that I think is more biblical. Some prophecies of judgment were fulfilled in a quite literal way in the destruction of Israel and Judah in 722 and 586 BC. Some prophecies of restoration had a similar fulfilment in the return from exile after 538 BC. But all these fulfilments in the history of the people of the Old Testament were partial and lacked the full impact of the prophecies; they were really only pale shadows of what had been predicted.[4] In Israel's history, the judgment was not as heavy as some of the prophecies seemed to indicate, and the restoration lacked the full

3. Eschatology is the technical term meaning the end or last things (Greek: *eschatos*, last).
4. Even in the Old Testament it is recognized that past historical fulfilments do not exhaust the prophecies. So Daniel extends the 70 years of Jeremiah to 'seventy weeks' (Dan. 9:2, 20–27). The post-exilic prophets all point to the need for a 'real' fulfilment in the future.

glory of the kingdom of God promised by the prophets. Only when we get to the New Testament is it maintained that the real fulfilment is at hand through the person and work of Jesus of Nazareth. The New Testament, then, shows us that the events of the earthly ministry of Jesus, including his death, resurrection and ascension followed by Pentecost, all determine the understanding of prophetic fulfilment.[5] There are enough specific examples of how the New Testament writers saw prophecy being fulfilled, and enough general principles laid down about how the kingdom comes, to allow us to understand the following structure:

- All prophecy is fulfilled at the first coming of Jesus in his life, death, and resurrection.
- All prophecy is being fulfilled in this present age as the gospel brings the elect into the kingdom of God by faith.
- All prophecy will be consummatively fulfilled in the whole universe when Jesus returns in glory to judge the living and the dead.

If this is a valid assessment, as I believe it is, then we must recognize that the biblical principle for the interpretation of prophecy is not a literalistic one. The New Testament defines it in terms of Jesus Christ: the principle is Christological.

Thus, although we use the word eschatology to refer to 'the last things', the eschatology of the prophets refers to what happened in the person and work of Jesus, to what is now happening among the people of God in the world, and to what will happen in the whole creation when Christ returns. To put it simply: all prophecy is fulfilled in the coming of Jesus, who comes in three ways. He came in the flesh in the gospel event. Then he came in his Spirit at Pentecost to indwell his church. Finally, he will come in glory to judge the living and the dead. Prophetic eschatology, then, is not of interest to us solely because it tells what will happen one day, but

---

5. I discuss in more detail the nature of prophetic fulfilment in my books *According to Plan* (Leicester: Inter-Varsity Press, 1991) and *Preaching the Whole Bible as Christian Scripture* (Grand Rapids: Eerdmans; Leicester: Inter-Varsity Press, 2000).

because it tells us about the three comings of Jesus and how we relate to them. What the prophets tell us about prayer is of significance because it applies first to Jesus, and then to us in the here and now. We are those 'on whom the end of the ages has come' (1 Cor. 10:11).

Because prophetic eschatology has its primary reference in Jesus, we may expect that its teaching on prayer will assist us to understand the significance of the prayers of Jesus. Furthermore, we are 'in Christ' and are thus defined by him. By learning of him, we learn of ourselves as those who have union with him. What was fulfilled for us in him is now in the process of being fulfilled in us. What was fulfilled in him two thousand years ago, and is now being fulfilled in us, will reach its consummation at his return. In other words, while all prophecy is fulfilled in three ways – in Christ, in us, and in the whole creation – we must distinguish these three modes of fulfilment and understand how they relate. The reason we can apply the psalms, the prophets or any of the Old Testament writings to ourselves is that they apply first and foremost to Jesus. We, then, are defined by sharing with him what belongs to his humanity. As yet we share it by imputation. This imputation of the righteousness of Christ is the basis of the fruit of the Spirit in us as we are more and more conformed to the image of Christ.

Prayer in prophetic eschatology

What does all this have to do with prayer? Before we can answer that we need to investigate the relevant texts from the prophetic books to see what emphasis and teaching on prayer they contain. We have observed some of those passages relating to the ministries of the prophets in their own time, such as the letter of Jeremiah. But eschatology stresses the future events of judgment and salvation, especially the final events of the age. Up to this point we have observed how the Old Testament emphasizes the role in prayer of the special ministers of God. Not until we come to the psalms is there any real consideration of prayer as a common function of all the people of God, and even that was qualified by the fact that most of the prayers are identified as prayers of the king.

In order to assess the place of prayer in prophetic eschatology, we need to recognize that, as in some psalms, little distinction is made between worship, singing to God, praising him, and calling upon him. These would all seem to be aspects of addressing God, directly or indirectly. We have followed this pattern in Christian worship.[6] When a congregation sings, 'Now thank we all our God', who is being addressed? The words of this hymn suggest that we are addressing each other, since God is spoken of in the third person. Yet it is unimaginable that the intention was anything else than to lift our hearts to God in thanksgiving.

An examination of prophetic eschatology yields the following themes:

The Day of the Lord

The prophets agree that a day is coming when God will perform a significant act of judgment and salvation. Some refer to this day as the Day of the Lord.[7] Sometimes the reference is to 'on that day'[8] or 'days are coming'.[9] Whether the prophet speaks of the imminent events relating to the Babylonian exile and return, or of a more distant and more comprehensive, even universal, judgment-redemption, the day is a significant one in the relationship of God to his people. Prayer is not directly mentioned in many of these references, but is often implied. Thus, on that day, 'the remnant of Israel . . . will lean on the LORD, the Holy One of Israel, in truth' (Is. 10:20), the Gentiles will seek the Lord on account of his saving activity in Israel (Is. 11:10–11), and even the Egyptians will swear allegiance to the Lord (Is. 19:18). The opening of Isaiah 25 indicates praise to God for the salvation to

---

6. Worship, strictly speaking, involves the whole of the Christian life. Here I am using it with the common meaning of what we do in a church service. Unfortunately the word has more recently been removed even further from its New Testament meaning to designate only the part of a service devoted to the singing of religious songs.
7. Is. 13:6, 9; Jer. 46:10; Ezek. 13:5; 30:3; Joel 1:15; 2:1, 11, 31; 3:14; Amos 5:20; Zeph. 1:7, 14; Mal. 4:5.
8. This phrase is found over eighty times in the prophetic books.
9. In Is. 39:6 the reference is to the coming exile into Babylon; in Jer. 51:47 the day is the day of judgment on Babylon.

come. Later, there is praise and rejoicing for salvation (Is. 25:9). One of the great songs of praise occurs in Isaiah 26. It moves between direct address to God and speaking about him, but verses 7–19 are a sustained song of praise. In similar strain is the exultation of the people in the Holy One of Israel (Is. 29:19). It is noteworthy that on that day God will write his covenant on the hearts of his people (Jer. 31:31–34). This covenant is the way people know the Lord (v. 34), for he reveals his nature and his saving love by this means. Knowing God means being in covenant relationship with him. As we have seen in the previous chapters that prayer and the covenant go together, so it becomes clearer that knowing God and prayer go together.

Prayers of repentance before the Day of the Lord

This dimension in prayer is clearly important. John the Baptist prepared the people for Jesus' ministry through his preaching and baptism of repentance (Matt. 3:1–6). Malachi promised that Elijah would come in this manner before the Day of the Lord (Mal. 4:5–6). Other prophets anticipated this aspect of the coming salvation by themselves praying the penitential prayer, or by forecasting the day when the people would approach God in this way, confessing their sins. Thus Isaiah bewails the condition of the people who are like those 'not called by your name' (Is. 63:15–19). Isaiah calls on God to 'tear open the heavens and come down', so that all may tremble at his judgments. He confesses the sins of his people and prays that judgment be averted (Is. 64:1–12). In the following oracle of the new creation God promises, 'Before they call I will answer; while they are yet speaking I will hear' (Is. 65:24). Jeremiah's letter to the Babylonian exiles speaks of how God will let them pray to him: they will find him if they seek with all their heart (Jer. 29:13–14). This indicates a change of heart in their coming to God; a true repentance.

People will seek the Lord and call upon him

The Old Testament evangel comes in many forms. It is a proclamation or heralding of good things that God will do in saving his people. Isaiah 55 puts this 'gospel' announcement in the form of the cry of a market vendor. He calls on people to take advantage of the gracious opportunity that is presented. It is the day of salvation and God has come near to them. They are urged to seek him and to call upon him; to return to a merciful God (Is. 55:6–7). Similarly, the invitation is given through Jeremiah: 'Call to me and I will answer you' (Jer. 33:3). That the Lord will draw near to his people and hear them is also a feature of this aspect of prayer. 'Then you shall call, and the LORD will answer; you shall cry, and he will say, "Here I am"' (Is. 58:9a). This will be so different from the time of Israel's rebellion when the Lord's readiness to be sought out was met with stubborn silence (Is. 65:1). God will remove profane speech and enable people to call on his name and to truly serve him (Zeph. 3:9, 14–20).

The fulfilment of the covenant promises of God

The covenant theme is a vital part of the whole perspective on prayer and the grace of the Lord as portrayed by the prophets. Again Isaiah 55 is an important chapter that combines so many of the central themes relating to prayer and redemption. The one reference to calling upon the Lord (v. 6) should not be allowed to obscure its context. The evangel is based on the covenant, here expressed as the promises to David (v. 3). This is at the heart of the ministry of Israel to the nations (v. 4–5); when Israel is saved this will bring the nations to know the Lord also. Calling upon the Lord can only be done along with repentance of sin (v. 7). The agent of all these events is the word of the Lord that cannot fail (v. 11). Finally, this evangel in which the people of God are involved through calling on him and being saved brings regeneration to the world of nature (vv. 12–13). It would not be an exaggeration to say that the Day of the Lord means the day on which the covenant is given its final expression through redemption. Isaiah issues an invitation to all the ends of the earth to be saved, for God says that all shall swear to the Lord while the offspring of Israel triumph and glory (Is. 45:22–25). The covenant will be fulfilled in such a way that the redeemed will not turn from God (Jer. 31:31–34; 32:37–41; 33:14–18; 50:4–5; Hos. 2:16–23).

The temple as God's house of prayer

As we might expect, the temple is found at the heart of oracles concerning the prayer of the redeemed people of God. Since the time of Solomon, the temple was the focal point of God's relationship with his people. In succession with the tabernacle, the temple was the place designated as the dwelling of God, the place where his name dwells, and the centre of the priestly ministry of reconciliation with God through sacrifice. Again direct references to prayer are few, but the dedicatory prayer of Solomon reminds us that reconciliation and fellowship with God are not wordless conditions. Prayer would figure very strongly in the temple. It was, therefore, the house of prayer (Is. 56:7). Thus, when Isaiah portrays the renewed temple in Zion as the place to which the nations will come to be taught the ways of the Lord, we must suppose that prayer would figure in this (Is. 2:2–4; 27:12–13). Often the temple is implied by the references to Zion. The significance of Zion as the name of Jerusalem, the holy city of God, is that the temple is there and the Davidic kingship rules from there. Thus to seek the Lord in Zion is to come to the temple on the basis of God's covenant promises. Practically all these themes are found in Jeremiah's oracle:

> In those days and in that time, declares the LORD, the people of Israel and the people of Judah shall come together, weeping as they come, and they shall seek the LORD their God. They shall ask the way to Zion, with faces turned toward it, saying, 'Come, let us join ourselves to the LORD in an everlasting covenant that will never be forgotten.'
>
> (Jer. 50:4–5)

The new song

Since we are including the notion of praising God as part of the scenario of prayer, it is worth noting the theme of the *new song*. The phrase occurs some nine times in the Bible: six in the psalms of praise, once in Isaiah, and twice in Revelation.[10] It is not unreasonable to suggest concerning the latter that John has taken up a theme of the Old Testament and that here it is given its fuller theological application that helps us to understand what is new about the song. In Revelation 5:9–10, the twenty-four elders, who seem to represent the people of God, sing a new song:

> Worthy are you to take the scroll
> and to open its seals,

10. Ps. 33:3; 40:3; 96:1; 98:1; 144:9; 149:1; Is. 42:10; Rev. 5:9; 14:3.

> for you were slain, and by your blood you ransomed people for God
> from every tribe and language and people and nation,
> and you have made them a kingdom and priests to our God,
> and they shall reign on the earth.

Then, in Revelation 14:1–5 John describes his vision of one hundred and forty-four thousand redeemed people on Mount Zion who sing a new song before the throne of God. Only the redeemed could learn this new song. In the Psalms and Isaiah, the new song is a song of redemption. It is new because the redemption being spoken of far outweighs the historic expression of it in the exodus from Egypt. Insofar as praise is prayer, this theme points to the exercising of prayer as something that stems from the experience of being saved. The content of the new song in Revelation 5 indicates that it consists of praise to the Lamb on the specific grounds of his saving activity.

Prophecy and the knowledge of God

It might be argued that, by taking material from the Hebrew scriptures alone, I have predetermined the outcome in terms of prayer to the God of the covenant. This is of course true. However, it should be noted that the biblical narrative from start to finish is exclusivist in that it allows for no other religion or gods as valid foci of reality. Prayer belongs to those in Christ because in Christ alone is there salvation. Only in Christ is there the truth about God and the universe. Only in Christ is there hope for all the peoples of the world. The prophetic view is that the events of the Day of the Lord include the coming of the nations to worship Yahweh, the Lord, at the temple in Zion. This is consistent with the biblical account of the universal significance of the God of Abraham, Isaac, Jacob and Jesus. Israel shall 'have no other gods before me' because there *are* no other gods. Israel's God made all that there is, established the rules and provided a way to escape his judgment for all the nations of the world. The pattern is that he chose Israel as his people, and promised that through them a blessing would come to all peoples (Gen. 12:1–3). This promise is at the heart of the prophetic message, the apostolic gospel, and the consummation at Christ's return. It forms the heart of the biblical theology of missionary endeavour. The nations will know God as the God who promised to Abraham that through his descendants all the nations of the earth shall be blessed.

I have laboured this point somewhat only because of the modern prevalence of an attitude of what is mistakenly called tolerance. This tolerant way of thinking is usually very intolerant of those who dare to suggest that Christ is the only saviour and, consequently, the only mediator of prayer to God. It must be admitted that, whatever the attitude people have to these claims, the biblical picture is marvellously consistent. Multiculturalism always places strains on exclusivism. While our society loves to see interfaith activities, only adherents of a pluralistic form of their religion will welcome participation in such expressions.[11] Christians will always be under pressure to pray publicly only in a form that involves the glaring omission of the name of Jesus or any Christian distinctives.

But the position set out in the prophets of Israel was quite distinctive. It was not that only Israel deserved the favour of God; the very opposite is true.[12] Having been favoured, the nation turns its back continually on the grace of God. So God will act one day to change all that. He will give to a chosen remnant of his people a new heart and spirit so that they will turn to him in repentance and faith. Then the nations of the world will see the gracious saving acts of God and come and seek him with Israel. They will come to the temple on Mount Zion and attach themselves to the saved people of Israel. The New Testament never loses sight of this perspective of salvation 'to the Jew first' (Rom. 1:16).

Prayer in the prophetic view of the coming salvation continues to lay the foundations for the New Testament expressions of the

11. Few adherents of any religion would accept the idea that all other religions are the same as theirs. It is rightly seen as an impossible proposition. World views of the different religions are, on the whole, totally incompatible. Every thinking person adopts their religious stance, including rationalism or atheism, because they believe they are right. Obviously if they didn't think so, they would adopt another position.

12. See Deut. 7:7–8.

exclusive mediatorial role of Jesus of Nazareth. The themes we have looked at above highlight both the exclusivist and the universalist dimensions. Yahweh alone is God; besides him there is none other. As Psalm 135:17 points out, to pray to another is to pray to an idol without ears. Yet the inevitable outcome of God's sovereign grace is that there will be 'a great multitude . . . from every nation, from all tribes and peoples and languages, standing before the throne and before the Lamb' (Rev. 7:9). The themes we have examined add up to this: on the Lord's day the covenant promises of God will be fulfilled in such a way that the hearts and minds of his people will be truly turned to him, first in repentance, and then in joyful praise for salvation. The redeemed people of God will worship before him in the new temple in the new Jerusalem, Jew and Gentile together. Some may need reminding that the new temple in the New Testament is first of all Jesus himself. We recognize, then, that the present-day missionary activity of the church is a fulfilment in these last days of the ingathering of the nations to the new temple.[13]

One further characteristic stands out in the present fulfilment of prophecy. As the prophets did then, so now we long for the consummation. Unlike the prophets who looked forward, we look back to the definitive fulfilment in Christ. The prophets give us a dynamic picture of a process that occurs on the Day of the Lord. This will be the time for people to seek the Lord and to come to him in repentant prayer. They will be saved whilst living in the midst of a sinful generation and in a strife-torn world. I want to emphasize that the New Testament perspective is that the 'last days' are not confined to some short period just before Jesus returns. The last days came with Jesus' first coming and will characterize our present age until Jesus returns in glory. I find that many people, especially those brought up on a diet of eschatology, find it difficult to grasp this point. My references above to the threefold fulfilment of prophecy need careful attention. The one coming of the Lord foreseen by the prophets is fulfilled in three ways: the first coming of Christ (gospel event), his coming by

13. See Graeme Goldsworthy, 'The Great Indicative: An Aspect of a Biblical Theology of Mission', *Reformed Theological Review*, 55, no. 1, 1996, pp. 2–13.

his Spirit beginning at Pentecost (this present age of proclamation of the gospel), and his second coming at the consummation of the promises (glorification of the church).

Thus, in these last days of Christ's presence by his gospel and Spirit, the petitions of the Lord's Prayer remain relevant since we are in this world and longing for the next. We continue to praise and worship God and to confess our sins. We pray for our daily bread and ask for protection against the evil that is all around us. With the psalmist we cry, 'How long, O Lord?' With John we dare to say, 'Come, Lord Jesus.' This longing is for the consummation when we shall see him face to face in the heavenly Jerusalem. Here there will be no death, tears or pain, for all things will be made new (Rev. 21:1–5). Satan will have been consigned to judgment in hell (Rev. 20:10).[14] Now there is endless praise, for God's kingdom, in the fullest possible sense, has come.

Summary

- Prophetic eschatology presents a view of a future glorious restoration of the nation and institutions of Israel. The New Testament declares the fulfilment of this restoration in Christ.
- The prophets emphasize certain themes centred on the prayers of repentance of a faithful remnant of Israel who will seek the Lord and call upon him.
- This prayer activity focuses on the nature of God as the Saviour who is faithful to his covenant promises.
- The temple is seen as central to the redemption as God's house of prayer and the place where the redeemed sing a new song of joyful praise.

---

14. This scenario is very different from the caricature in comic strips and cartoons depicting Satan and the demons in charge of the torment of people consigned to that place. Hell, in biblical terms, is first and foremost the place where Satan and the demons meet their destruction under the judgment of God.

Pause a moment . . .

Reflect on how the prophets' perspectives on prayer help us to put meaning into the petition 'Your kingdom come' when we pray the Lord's Prayer.

Think about the global view of the prophetic eschatology and its implication for the focus of our prayers:

- in praise and thanksgiving for the saving work of Christ
- for mission
- for perseverance in faith until Christ comes again.

10 The progress of prayer IV. The New Testament

The time is fulfilled

We have now come full circle. We began with Jesus in the Gospels as they recount aspects of his ministry in his life, death and resurrection. It was necessary to consider the foundational significance for prayer of the ascension of Jesus to heaven and his continuous priestly intercession for the people of God. Now that we have examined the background to this in the way prayer is revealed in the various stages of the Old Testament, we are in a better position to understand why the emphases in the New Testament teaching on prayer are what they are. At the start of his ministry, Jesus proclaimed, 'The time is fulfilled, and the kingdom of God is at hand; repent and believe in the gospel' (Mark 1:14–15). The reference to fulfilment indicates that Jesus understood his ministry as bringing the Old Testament ministries to their full realization. The four Gospel writers tell us in a number of places that Jesus acted or spoke to fulfil the Scriptures or the prophets' pronouncements. If we apply this to the subject of prayer, which indeed we must, we find that it implies a great deal more than the assertions that Jesus was a teacher who instructed his disciples about prayer, and that he gave us an example to follow.

Since I have discussed in some detail certain aspects of Jesus' teaching on prayer and his intercession for his people,[1] it is necessary here only to summarize a few main points. What we have observed in examining the whole background to prayer – its reality, its grounds, its source and its enabling – is that the nature of authentic prayer first and foremost reflects the nature of God. Thus prayer and our knowledge of God are inseparable. And since God is revealed as Trinity, it is impossible to understand the biblical view of prayer apart from the appreciation of God as Trinity. Prayer is intimately related to the redemption we have through the gospel of Christ, and the gospel can only be the way it is because God is Trinity. We also noted that the whole gospel transaction is carried out on the basis of the Second Person of the Trinity becoming a human being and restoring all things *in himself* before ever we become involved. The fulfilment of the Old Testament takes place in Jesus Christ before it affects us as Christian believers. All that the Old Testament teaches about the activity of God, and about the roles of the covenant functionaries (prophets, priests and kings), can only have relevance to us because it is fulfilled in Jesus to whom we are then united by faith.

What did the Old Testament reveal about the nature of prayer? First, in the history of the Old Testament people we observed that the main emphasis was on the special ministers as those who prayed to God on behalf of the people. This, we saw, did not imply that ordinary people let the 'clergy' do all the praying for them, but was a way of showing the central importance of the mediators of God's saving grace and kingly rule when it came to the matter of prayer. Prayer, in other words, is not, and never has been since Adam sinned, a direct hotline to heaven. It is always a mediated thing; there has to be a fitting go-between if we are to communicate with God. Those who reject the mediator reject prayer as it is intended to be. God makes himself known to his people within the framework of his covenant, and prayer is contingent upon this covenant relationship between God and his people.

Second, in the Psalms we saw the same emphasis on the covenant ministers as mediators, as well as more specific indications of prayer

1. See chapter 3.

in the lives of the ordinary men and women of God. Because the special ministers were representatives of the whole population, there is no fixed barrier between ministers and people. When the prophets, the priests or the kings expressed their ministries in prayer, all the people of God were involved in that prayer. Many psalms make sense as the utterances of the godly man or woman without ever implying that mediation was done away with. The book of Psalms also assists us by showing the major types of prayer that were seen to be appropriate responses to the God who had revealed himself to Israel. Thus the psalms show how we can move from lamentations for sin or because of persecution and other suffering to prayers for deliverance, to thanksgivings for the mercies of God, including salvation, and then to joyous praise of God who has revealed his faithfulness to his covenant promises in redeeming his people. In the Psalms, the covenantal relationship of those who pray to God is constantly and explicitly before us in terms of God's steadfast love or covenant faithfulness.

Third, in the prophetic eschatology we saw how certain prominent themes emerge that express the nature and direction of prayer as God moves finally to bring in his kingdom. The prophets look for the Day of the Lord, when salvation will be revealed in all its fullness. This will be a day when people are moved to repent and to confess their sins. Jew and Gentile alike will come to the Lord and call on him. Then the new covenant will be written on the hearts of God's people and they will know the Lord. At this time all the covenant promises of God will be fulfilled. Those who seek God will do so at his temple on Zion. There they will sing a new song that only the redeemed can know and utter.

When we looked at the Gospel narratives concerning prayer, we observed that there is a transition from the situation in the Old Testament to that which pertains after the ascension of Jesus. In the Gospel accounts of his earthly ministry, Jesus shows that he is the fulfiller of all Old Testament Scriptures. This indicates that the end of the age, the last days, arrived at Jesus' first coming. We would expect this perspective to be demonstrated in the way prayer is dealt with after Pentecost. Pentecost, the giving of the Holy Spirit, marks the point at which the apostles and the other disciples of Jesus began to preach the full gospel. In the Old Testament the gospel was foreshadowed by the acts of God in Israel's history as God himself interpreted these events. Nearly a thousand years elapsed from the time God gave the covenant promises to Abraham until they received a comprehensive fulfilment in Israel's history. Solomon's building of the temple marks a high point in the realization of the covenant promises, and it was at that time that both wisdom and prayer reach correspondingly high watermarks.

It is no surprise, then, that the coming of the One who is 'greater than Solomon', the true Son of David, who is himself the new and glorious temple, should also mark a new high point in both wisdom and prayer. Jesus' teaching on prayer, and his practice of it, recall in various ways the foundations laid in the Old Testament. However, there is a new element in that now the true mediator is being revealed. The Old Testament ministers were 'types' of Christ; the nature of their ministries foreshadowed the ministry of Jesus. Their ministries had authenticity and effectiveness only insofar as they pointed forward to the ministry of Jesus. What Jesus was and did had an efficacy that reached back, through these foreshadowing 'types', into the past history of God's people. Through the Holy Spirit's ministry in relation to the apostolic word, Jesus' ministry also reaches forward to this present age. The high priestly prayer of Jesus in John 17 links the situation of his disciples with his eternal glory as it once was, and as it is soon to be again. We have looked at some of the places in the epistles that speak of the ongoing high priestly ministry of Jesus in heaven. It now remains only to consider something of the way the New Testament instructs us about our prayer between Pentecost and the return of Jesus.

Prayer in the Acts of the Apostles

Although the narrative of Acts is mostly concerned with events after Pentecost, there is still some value in treating it as distinct from the rest of the New Testament documents that are addressed to the post-Pentecost church. This is because Acts shows us that there is a period of transition from the way things were when Jesus was present in the flesh with his disciples to the period in which we now live: between Pentecost and the return of Christ. None of the New Testament documents will address us exactly as if written to us today. One major difference is that the individual New Testament documents come from the apostolic age before the canon of Scripture was fully formed or recognized. But in Acts the situation is even more fluid. First, for the disciples, the full significance of the ascension of Jesus and of the coming of the Holy Spirit took a while to sink in, particularly with regard to the inclusion of the Gentiles under the covenant blessings of God. However, we would expect the apostles and those with them to be responding to the new situation with insights granted by the Holy Spirit himself, since Jesus promised that the Spirit would lead them into all truth.

Direct references in Acts to the apostolic church and prayer include the following categories:

- The fact that they prayed, but without specifying the content of their prayers (Acts 1:14; 3:1; 6:4; 9:11; 10:9, 30; 11:5; 20:36; 21:5; 22:17).
- Prayer for guidance (Acts 1:24).[2]
- Prayer for deliverance in times of danger or threat (Acts 4:24–31; 12:5, 12; 16:25).
- Prayer when commissioning ministers (Acts 6:6; 13:3; 14:23).
- Prayer for healing or welfare (Acts 9:40; 26:29; 28:8).
- Prayer for certain specific outsiders to receive the Holy Spirit so that they might become part of the body of believers (Acts 8:15; 19:6).[3]
- Prayer in relation to a God-fearer, that is a Gentile who had converted to Judaism or was in the process of doing so (Acts 10:2, 4, 30). The Christian Jews had great difficulty in coming to terms with the blessing of the non-Jew Cornelius. Yet this was a clear fulfilment of the Old Testament Scriptures that the Gentiles would come to

---

2. It should be noted that the use of a lottery to choose the new apostle took place before the coming of the Holy Spirit and that, after Pentecost, there is no evidence that it was ever used again as a method of guidance.
3. Both of these are unique events and should not be used to establish the idea of a separate baptism of the Spirit after conversion. The history of the Samaritans made it necessary for the Jewish apostles to administer the blessing lest the Samaritan schism continue in the church. The Ephesians clearly needed to hear the full gospel in order to receive the Spirit. The context of this reference to the laying on of hands would seem to imply that prayer was offered.

Zion.[4] The fact that Cornelius had adopted the Jewish faith before he was converted is not the key issue, but it does suggest that he probably already understood something of the need for the ministry of mediation if his prayer was to be accepted.

- Praise for God's marvellous deeds (Acts 2:46–47; 3:8).

There are also some indirect clues to prayer in the calling on people to repent, which would involve them in calling on the name of the Lord (Acts 2:21, 38; 3:19; 8:22).

These prayers reflect the struggle that the first Christians had to adapt to a new perspective brought about by the ministry, death, resurrection and ascension of Jesus. It was a struggle to grasp the eschatological nature of their time. The human struggle is apparent in the way they found it hard to let go of the temple in Jerusalem, and in the even greater difficulty they had in accepting that God was bringing Gentiles into his church. Both should have been obvious from the Old Testament Scriptures when interpreted in the light of Christ's person and work, but the human heart is slow to accept such changes. The gospel framework that Jesus brought was not in itself difficult, but the paradigm shift from the traditional Jewish perceptions of how the kingdom of God would come involved a massive change of perspective. They now had to cope with the fact that all the promises of the covenant focused, not upon the literal land of Israel, Jerusalem and the temple, but upon Jesus as the fulfiller of all these things.

Prayer in the Pauline epistles[5]

Our investigation of prayer in the various stages of Old Testament revelation has revealed that prayer is a function of the covenant

4. The original promise to Abraham in Genesis 12:3 is given substance by the prophets and their expectations for the future coming of the kingdom; e.g. Is. 2:2–4; Zech. 8:20–23.
5. While there is some scholarly dispute over which of the epistles were actually written by Paul, I am accepting the Pauline authorship of those bearing his name. This is a convenient division of the New Testament documents since I am not trying to establish the Pauline distinctives in his view of prayer.

relationship between God and his people. This relationship is primarily that by which people are justified and made the people of God. It was in response to the covenant promises that 'he [Abraham] believed the LORD, and he counted it to him as righteousness' (Gen. 15:6). The covenant, moreover, signifies the way for people to have friendship with God and to know him. Thus Abraham is referred to as the friend of God (2 Chr. 20:7; Is. 41:8; Jas. 2:23). The Lord spoke to Moses as to a friend (Exod. 33:11). Job experienced the friendship of God (Job 29:4). The psalmist understands the friendship of the Lord as belonging to those who fear him (Ps. 25:14). He thus recognizes that reverent obedience of the Lord is required under the covenant. Jesus reinforced this covenant notion of friendship with God as he showed his disciples that their relationship with him was friendship with God (John 15:14–15). This changing of the disciples' designated relationship from servants to friends does not imply that friendship with God is a totally new emphasis, but rather that the significance of their relationship with Jesus needs some clarification. Let us remember that the friendship of Jesus with his disciples is a profound relationship that they are privileged to have with the living Word of God. What emerges in this is that the knowledge of God is not to be mistaken for some mystical inner feeling of being in touch with the divine. It is, rather, a relationship of knowing God's word and responding to it with obedience and faith. As our explicit knowledge of God's word grows, so we have the grounds for an explicit knowledge of God himself. God's word, illumined by the Holy Spirit, is the means by which God makes himself present to us. Some theologians have made a sharp distinction between the idea of God communicating truth about himself in the Bible and God communicating himself. They deny that the Bible contains the truth about God and yet say that God offers himself through this medium. This separation of knowledge about God and personal relationship with him is unsustainable, as both are clearly true.[6]

In the New Testament, fellowship (Gk. *koinōnia*) becomes a

---

6. This is dealt with in Leon Morris, *I Believe in Revelation* (London: Hodder and Stoughton, 1976), especially in chapter 6.

gospel-enhanced notion of the covenant relationship. The idea of fellowship expresses the relationship that exists between the people of God, but this is a covenantal relationship. It has its basis in the fellowship we have with God through the covenant relationship that is achieved for us in Christ. God has called us into the fellowship of his Son (1 Cor. 1:9). Paul's desire was that 'I may know him and the power of his resurrection, and may share [*koinōnia*] his sufferings' (Phil. 3:10). For John, by sharing what he had seen and heard of Jesus, the Word of life, he enabled his hearers to have fellowship with himself. The reality behind this Christian fellowship is made clear: 'Indeed our fellowship is with the Father and with his Son Jesus Christ' (1 John 1:3). But this fellowship is dependent on their walking in the light of the knowledge of God (1 John 1:6–7). In turning to the letters of Paul we note that three main aspects present themselves with regard to prayer: expressed wishes that imply Paul's prayer for his readers; actual instruction on prayer; and a recounting of the content of Paul's prayers or of the prayers of others.[7]

Paul's implied prayer

By implied prayer I mean those expressions that are directly addressed to the readers but imply a prayer that Paul makes on their behalf. He has a distinctive but flexible form of initial greeting, which varies in length and content but is always followed by the prayerful wish: 'Grace to you and peace from God our Father and the Lord Jesus Christ.' In Colossians and 1 Thessalonians this greeting of grace is shortened, and it is slightly lengthened in 2 Timothy, Titus and Philemon. These variations are not significant enough to warrant an attempt to explain them. A number of the letters repeat the grace at the end. The common feature is that Paul expressed his prayer that the addressees would continue to experience the grace and peace of God. Other prayerful desires are framed in the more complete form of the wish that something would be the case. Thus, in 1 Thessalonians 3:11–12 we have:

---

7. A detailed analysis of the subject is given in W. B. Hunter, 'Prayer', in G. F. Hawthorne and R. P. Martin (eds.), *Dictionary of Paul and His Letters* (Downers Grove: InterVarsity Press; Leicester: Inter-Varsity Press, 1993).

> Now may our God and Father himself, and our Lord Jesus, direct our way to you, and may the Lord make you increase and abound in love for one another and for all, as we do for you.

If we are not to dismiss these expressions as mere social graces, formalities that are little more than polite greetings, then we must assume that they carried the weight of a covenant of prayer. They are not expressions of wishful thinking but rather imply the mutual responsibility of prayer that goes with the fellowship that we have with one another in Christ. The content of the implied prayer is also important. Words such as grace and peace are not up for grabs to be interpreted by common English usage. They are shorthand terms for gospel truths. Thus, grace is the word that covers the undeserved mercy of God that underlies the saving work of Christ and our being made his co-heirs of the kingdom. Peace is not an inner calm and serenity (although it may from time to time produce this effect), but our reconciliation with the God we have offended by our rebellion against him.

Paul's instruction about prayer

Instruction about prayer includes both theological analysis of the nature of prayer and practical exhortations. Paul gives instructions about the conduct of prayer in the assembly, and also urges his readers to persevere in this fundamental activity. The combined effect is to highlight the fact that prayer is an expression of our relationship with God, so that both the divine and the human roles need to be considered. A number of aspects of prayer emerge in Paul's teaching.

Instructions to pray[8]

It is clear that Paul understands that perseverance in prayer is not always easy. He understands all too well the weakness of the flesh that works against continuing in prayer. That is why it is necessary to exhort one another to maintain some kind of discipline of prayer.

---

8. Rom. 12:12; 1 Cor. 7:5; Phil. 4:4–6; Col. 4:2; 1 Thess. 5:16–21; 1 Tim. 2:1; 5:5.

The effects of prayer[9]

In Romans 10:12–13, Paul echoes the evangelistic reference to prayer of Joel 2:32, which was also quoted by Peter in Acts 2:21 and which recalls the foundational prayer reference in Genesis 4:26. The Joel passage, as we have seen, points us to the Day of the Lord and the salvation that comes to all who call upon him. The knowledge that the believers pray for him is also a source of strength and confidence for Paul. His suffering in imprisonment is greatly alleviated because he is confident that the Philippian Christians are praying for him (Phil. 1:19).

Requests for prayer[10]

It is clear that Paul understands that praying for others in the body of Christ is an aspect of fellowship. It is a means of fellowship that transcends the need for physical proximity. He understands it, in the way John does, to mean that our fellowship is with the Father and the Son. Thus, *in Christ*, we have fellowship one with another. An important theological truth underlies this fact. Human sin alienated us from God and from one another. Just as our fellowship with God is restored only through the mediation of Christ, so also our fellowship with one another exists only through him. This is what differentiates our relationships to other Christians from our relationships to non-Christians. Christian relationships are mediated through Christ. One principal way we have of both experiencing and expressing that fellowship is by prayer for one another.

Directions for the conduct of prayer[11]

These are not practical directions for running a prayer service or one's private devotions, but rather reflect the implications of Paul's theology of prayer. How we conduct prayer will show what we understand it to be. This in turn is a reflection of our knowledge of God.

---

9. Rom. 10:13; 2 Cor. 1:11; Phil. 1:19; 1 Tim. 4:5.

10. Rom. 15:30–32; 1 Thess. 5:25; 2 Thess. 3:1.

11. 1 Cor. 11:4–5; 14:13–19; Eph. 5:18–20; 6:18; 1 Tim. 2:8.

Eschatological prayer[12]

At the end of Paul's hymn on the exaltation of the servant Christ, found in Philippians 2:6–11, in verse 10 he refers to the effect of Christ's exaltation as causing everyone to bow to him and every tongue to confess that Jesus is Lord. That this takes place 'in heaven and on earth and under the earth' indicates that the time will come when those who are redeemed will confess him with joy, while those who have refused the redemptive love of Christ will acknowledge him in terror. This is entirely in keeping with the teaching of the prophets who speak of those under the judgment of God being forced to recognize 'That I am the LORD'. For example, Ezekiel frequently speaks of both redemption and judgment as that by which people will know him. Paul's perspective is also consistent with the teaching of Jesus. Thus Jesus relates the fate of those who will speak to him on the Day of Judgment to plead their cause, only to be rejected.[13] There are also references to the demons recognizing Jesus during his earthly ministry and shrinking from him.[14] Similarly, Jesus demonstrates his power to unbelieving Jews so that, 'you may know that the Son of Man has authority on earth to forgive sins' (Mark 2:9–10).

God's role in our prayer

The most significant passage in this regard is Paul's reference in Romans 8 to the work of the Holy Spirit as intercessor and helper in our prayers. This is not an easy passage, but we should not ignore Paul's use of the little connective word *likewise*. It seems that it connects the passage with the reference to creation and to believers who groan inwardly:

> For the creation waits with eager longing for the revealing of the sons of God. For the creation was subjected to futility, not willingly, but because of him who subjected it, in hope that the creation itself will be set free from its

---

12. While I have asserted the essentially eschatological nature of all prayer, we are concerned here with a situation that Paul understands as taking place at the consummation.
13. Matt. 7:21–23; Luke 16:19–31.
14. Mark 5:7–9; Luke 4:41.

> bondage to decay and obtain the freedom of the glory of the children of God. For we know that the whole creation has been groaning together in the pains of childbirth until now. And not only the creation, but we ourselves, who have the firstfruits of the Spirit, groan inwardly as we wait eagerly for adoption as sons, the redemption of our bodies.
>
> (Rom. 8:19–23)

> Likewise the Spirit helps us in our weakness. For we do not know what to pray for as we ought, but the Spirit himself intercedes for us with groanings too deep for words. And he who searches hearts knows what is the mind of the Spirit, because the Spirit intercedes for the saints according to the will of God.
>
> (Rom. 8:26–27)

The first part of this extraordinary statement is clearly eschatological. The creation is seen to be in travail with birth pains as its destiny is tied to the redemptive event set in motion by the death and resurrection of Christ. In the same way, the first fruits of the Spirit cause the redeemed people of God to groan inwardly in expectation of the fullness of salvation, which is the redemption of the whole person, including our bodies. Likewise the Spirit helps us in our weakness. John Calvin expresses it thus: 'We are bidden to knock. But no one of his own accord could premeditate a single syllable, unless God were to knock to gain admission to our souls by the secret impulse of His Spirit, and thus open our hearts to himself.'[15]

This last point bears further consideration. Paul's view of the Spirit, as with Jesus' understanding in his discourse in John 14 – 16, is that his ministry is to point us to Christ's person and work. That is, the Spirit does not do a work independent of that of the Son; Word and Spirit operate together. Paul's teaching about the Spirit's intercession for us in Romans 8:27 must be understood along with his previous statements about the Spirit in the same chapter. The Spirit-enabled prayer is thus prayer towards the eschatological goal revealed by the Father through the ministry of the Son. We see the goal but dimly. When we read the great passages of Scripture dealing

---

15. Calvin, *Commentary on Romans*, translated by Ross Mackenzie (Edinburgh: Oliver and Boyd, 1961), p. 178.

with the consummation of all God's purposes, our minds can scarcely take in such revelation about the glory yet to be revealed. The Spirit's enabling and his intercession for us do not magically fill in the gaps left purposely by God, but they take our longings to heaven. The Spirit will keep our gaze on the Lamb slain for us, and on his glorious resurrection and ascension. For the moment we live by faith, not by sight (2 Cor. 5:7). Yet the goal of our prayer is the consummation of all things in the new heaven and the new earth. Prayer can never be for the status quo. It does not seek to keep things as they are, but to engage the dynamic of the kingdom. The petition 'Your kingdom come' is the mark of Christian prayer! This future goal underlies even the mundane things we ask for, the details of our personal lives, the thanksgiving for past blessings, and praise for present provisions and for the sheer joy of knowing God.

Paul's instructions about prayer, then, indicate something of his understanding of the knowledge we have of God through the gospel, and of the relationship that belongs to all those who are redeemed in Christ. Paul's prayer is grounded firmly on his trinitarian theology and, as such, it points us to the fact that to know God is to know him both as he is in himself and as he acts towards us.

Paul's recounting of his actual prayer or the prayer of others

We can learn much from Paul's references to the content of his prayers. In the light of our investigations into the progress of prayer we would expect the apostle to exhibit a comprehensive understanding of the nature of prayer. We would also expect that Paul's conversion would bring a radical realignment of his prayers to the mediation of Jesus Christ.

Prayer relating to Paul's ministry and journeys

Paul had no doubt that his ministry involved both the sovereign working of God and his own responsibility to work faithfully. This is reflected in his references to prayers that he makes concerning the desire that he has to minister in various places. Thus he asks that he might be able to visit the churches in Rome and in Thessalonica.[16] He

16. Rom. 1:8–10; 1 Thess. 3:10.

requests prayer for his own success and safety in his journeys.[17] Paul also relates how he was moved to request God to remove his 'thorn in the flesh'.[18] There is no hint here of the triumphalism that we sometimes fall prey to. Our discussion on the relationship of prayer to faith is relevant here. Whatever Paul's affliction, it was made clear to him that it was not inconsistent with his status as a child of God. He had no lack of faith to repent of. Rather he had to learn afresh the lesson that the grace of God, his gospel, is sufficient for us. His prayer for relief received a kindly refusal, and he was redirected to the real fountainhead of strength in Christ. It is clear that some prayers are not granted, not because we lack faith, but because the sovereign will of God is expressed in another way. God has a wisdom that, from time to time, uses our suffering and even martyrdom for his glory. Whenever such an answer is received it throws us back onto trust in the goodness of God and the fact that he often chooses not to reveal the details of his plan for us.

Prayer for Israel to be saved

We cannot go into Paul's convictions about Israel in detail. Suffice it to say that it is clear that he not only longs for his own people to come to a knowledge of Christ, but that he also never loses sight of the covenant promises concerning this people.[19] This prayer for the salvation of Israel should not be confused with the idea, nowhere to be found in Paul, that this salvation involves a return to Palestine and some kind of millennial reign of Christ there. For Paul the gospel is 'to the Jew first' (Rom. 1:16), and the means of reaching the Gentiles is through the Jews who come to Christ. Thus, when he turns from the Jews to become the Apostle to the Gentiles, he goes to a synagogue because it is there that he will find the Gentile God-fearers

17. Rom. 15:30–32; 2 Thess. 3:1–2.

18. 2 Cor. 12:7–10.

19. See Donald Robinson, *Faith's Framework: The Structure of New Testament Theology* (Exeter: Paternoster; Sydney: Albatross, 1985), especially chapter 4. Also, G. Goldsworthy, 'Biblical Theology and the Shape of Paul's Mission', in Peter Bolt and Mark Thompson (eds.), *The Gospel to the Nations: Perspectives on Paul's Mission* (Leicester: Apollos; Downers Grove: InterVarsity Press, 2000).

(Acts 13:46–47; 14:1). This is the fulfilling of the covenant with Abraham (Gen. 12:3) and the prophecies of the Gentiles finding salvation (Is. 2:2–4; Zech. 8:20–23). Paul, of course, understands that Jerusalem and the temple are now in Christ, who is Israel's Messiah. Worship at the synagogue saves neither Jew nor Gentile; both need to come to Christ by faith and be made into 'one new man' in him (Eph. 2:11–22).

Prayer for the saints

The petitions that Paul makes for other Christians show us something of the dimensions of prayer, as he understands it. Thus, the somewhat complicated relationship with the Corinthian Christians that Paul deals with in the second epistle leads him to pray for them that they can rise to the challenge to understand his role as an apostle and the authority of his ministry (2 Cor. 13:5–10). He prays for their perfection or their maturity in sanctification. Paul's prayer for the Ephesian Christians expresses a similar eschatological goal (Eph. 1:16–23). Here Paul seems to merge a report on what he prays with a theological explanation of the significance of the prayer. He prays that God will give them a spirit of wisdom, and that they will be enlightened to know the nature of the hope they are called to, that is, the riches of their inheritance, and the greatness of God's power.[20] The important thing here is that this power that Paul wants them to know and understand is not an experience that we have, but rather it is the gospel event of the resurrection and exaltation of Jesus. This perspective is carried over into the status of the Christian in Christ that Paul expounds a little further on (Eph. 2:5–6). Clearly, Paul understands that our first need is to grasp in greater and greater depth the meaning of God's saving actions in Christ. In this same epistle Paul further prays that his readers will not be discouraged by his sufferings on their behalf (Eph. 3:13). He then goes on to pray for their spiritual strengthening, that Christ may dwell in their hearts by faith, that they might comprehend the immensity of Christ's love so

---

20. In vv. 20–23 we have an explanatory statement of the nature of this power of God. The NRSV makes a new sentence out of it, but the structure of the Greek, which makes this a relative clause, is better represented in the ESV.

that they might be filled with the fullness of God (Eph. 3:14–19). This indwelling of Christ is through the presence of the Spirit (v. 16), and it involves the power to comprehend Christ's love. Thus it is by faith; the Spirit gives faith in the person and work of Christ. To have Christ in their hearts is not somehow having the divine essence of Jesus in them. Nor is the heart the part of us that makes us feel good or have the 'warm fuzzies'. Paul's prayer is for them to be so focused on Christ with their whole being that they will be able to comprehend the greatness of his love, his person and his work.[21]

In Philippians 1:9–11 Paul's prayer for their present growth in love and knowledge is aimed at the eschatological outcome: that they might be blameless in the day of Christ having produced a harvest of righteousness. Similarly, in Colossians 1:9–10 the concern is for them to have a knowledge of God's will in spiritual wisdom and understanding. The goal is that they may lead fruitful lives worthy of the Lord. Quite simply, then, the common feature of Paul's reported intercessions for his Christian readers is that the gospel will continue to bear fruit in their lives, fruit that has significance for their ultimate destiny of eternal life.

Thanksgiving for the grace of God in his own life and in the lives of others

Paul is constantly thankful for the fruit of the gospel, whether as a result of his ministry or of other people's. He desires greatly to go to Rome, though he was denied this until his final journey. In the meantime he gives thanks for the faith of the Christians there (Rom. 1:8). He thanks God for the working of his own salvation in Christ (Rom. 7:25). He gives thanks for the Corinthian Christians because of the richness of the grace of God shown to them (1 Cor. 1:4–7). He is thankful to God for the faith of the Ephesian Christians and their love for all the saints (Eph. 1:15–16). The Philippian Christians are a cause of great joy and thanksgiving because they share in the gospel (Phil.

---

21. The real opposition is between mere outward appearances and genuine thinking leading to right action (so 2 Cor. 5:12). Paul has the Philippians in his heart (Phil. 1:7), which suggests that he holds them in affection and esteem, or that he is concerned for them.

1:3–5). He thanks God for the Colossians, for their faith, love and hope of heaven (Col. 1:3–5). He is similarly thankful for the Thessalonians and for Philemon (1 Thess. 1:2–3; 2 Thess. 1:3; Philem. 4–5). In the latter, it is clear that thanksgiving forms part of Paul's understanding of prayer; he does not see prayer as only petition, even though that is the primary sense of the word. More importantly, though, we see that Paul cannot address God with petition and as an expression of his fellowship with other Christians without at the same time giving voice to his sense of the amazing grace of God in the gospel.

The sum total of our investigation is that the way we pray should be a reflection of the God we know. Prayer is inseparable from knowing the God who has revealed himself. It is thus covenantal and eschatological. And since part of knowing God is knowing how his sovereignty works in relationship to our humanity, there are areas where prayer can only be the expression of our resignation in trust to the wisdom and goodness of God's plan for our lives and for the world.

Prayer in Hebrews and the general epistles

The references relating to prayer in Hebrews are few but significant. First, and of greatest importance, are the passages dealing with Jesus and his prayer. In view of our discussion of the foundations of prayer, it is worth noting that the epistle begins with a reference to the Son through whom God has spoken in these last days (Heb. 1:1–2). This sonship is known not only because of the word of God *through* the Son, but because of the word of God *to* the Son (Heb. 1:5–13). Then we see the word of the Son to the Father. The Son is then the one who makes acceptable intercession to the Father. In Hebrews 5:5–10 the prayers of Jesus during his earthly ministry are referred to in relation to his obedience in suffering and the salvation it achieved for us. His ministry is thus described as a high priesthood after the order of Melchizedek. This is a permanent ministry that is not hampered by the need that characterized the Old Testament priests to make constant sacrifices. His perpetual priesthood lies not in a repetition of his one true sacrifice, but in his being the perpetual mediator and intercessor on the basis of his once-for-all sacrifice (Heb. 7:23–25). Our High Priest mediates a better covenant than the old one that was but a shadow of the new. Now Jeremiah's prophecy of a new covenant is fulfilled in Christ who, on the behalf of believers, is the true people of God, truly knows God, and brings the forgiveness of sins (Heb. 8:1–13; 10:11–18).

This perfect ministry of Christ in his mediation of the new covenant, and his intercession for us, gives the believer confidence to approach God (Heb. 10:19–22). The encouragement to draw near to God is not specifically spoken of as involving prayer. It is more a matter of having confidence that we are accepted, the assurance of cleansing from pollution that would result in a bad conscience. It also has a community-directed aspect in that it results in mutual encouragement within the fellowship of believers (Heb. 10:23–25). But in view of the constant discourse that Hebrews describes as characterizing the relationship of the Father and the Son, it is almost inconceivable that this relationship we have to God under this new covenant would not involve a drawing near to God in prayer. If we can draw near to a personal, discoursing God through our discoursing High Priest and Mediator, then we will inevitably express this confidence in a personal way as Jesus did and continues to do for us in addressing the Father.

In the epistle of James the first reference to prayer is the advice to ask God for wisdom when it is lacking. We should understand this in the light of the wisdom ethos of the epistle. James contains a lot of practical advice in a way that suggests that he is well versed in the wisdom traditions of Israel. James deals with many of the practical themes of wisdom, and here he exhorts his reader to pray in faith for wisdom in the face of trials. The wisdom from above will be displayed by faith in action (Jas. 3:13–18). James shares the general perspective of the practical wisdom of the Old Testament in that it involves considered choices for actions that are consistent with the truth of God. Yet he is convinced of the role of prayer in this practical life. This is James' way of expressing the principle of Proverbs that 'the fear of the Lord is the beginning of wisdom' (Prov. 1:7; 9:10). We are dependent on the Lord for wisdom to live a life that is consistent with our profession, and we have prayer as a powerful and effective aid to deal with suffering and trials (Jas. 5:13–18).

Peter, like Paul, uses the grace formula to begin his letters. He has two explicit references to prayer, both in the first epistle. The first comes in a quote from Psalm 34 that he applies as a word of encouragement to behave consistently with the gospel in the face of suffering. It amounts to a reassurance that God's ears are open to the prayers of the righteous (1 Pet. 3:8–12). His second reference is an exhortation that, because we live at the end of the age, we should be serious and disciplined 'for the sake of your prayers' (1 Pet. 4:7). We lack any explanation of this charge, but it seems reasonable to deduce that Peter warns against all the perils and diversions of the age that would entice us to neglect fellowship with God and Christian service.

John's epistles contain few specific teachings on prayer. John has most to say in the last part of the first letter. Here he speaks of the boldness we have to ask anything according to his will and know that he hears us. The teaching here is similar to what Jesus teaches about prayer in faith and prayer in his name.[22] In 3 John 2 the author refers to his rather general prayer that things will go well with Gaius to whom the letter is addressed. Indirectly, John's assurance that confession of sins leads to forgiveness is presumably a reference to confession to God as well as, perhaps, to the assembly (1 John 1:9).

Prayer in the book of Revelation

There are two explicit references to prayer in Revelation: Revelation 5:8 and 8:3–5. We should be careful to try to understand the significance of these passages since the contexts in which they occur are really very important to John's message. Furthermore, John mentions the prayers of the saints without any explanatory comments, so that we are left to try to understand their significance from what is going on in these visions. The first occurs in what we must regard as a key passage in the message of the whole book. Revelation 5 describes John's vision of the throne in heaven and the problem of the scroll with seven seals. John is distressed because no-one could open the sealed scroll that, we may infer, contains the revelation of

22. This matter was discussed in chapter 5.

God's saving acts, his judgments and his kingdom.[23] One of the heavenly elders tells John that the Lion of the tribe of Judah is able to open the scroll, but when he looks to see this magnificent conquering beast he sees a Lamb standing 'as though it had been slain'. The Lamb, clearly the crucified Christ, takes the scroll and, as he does so, the four living creatures and the twenty-four elders fall before him, each holding a harp and bowls of incense, 'which are the prayers of the saints'. As they do so, they sing the new song:

> Worthy are you to take the scroll
>   and to open its seals,
> for you were slain, and by your blood you ransomed people for God
>   from every tribe and language and people and nation,
> and you have made them a kingdom and priests to our God,
>   and they shall reign on the earth.
>
> (Rev. 5:9–10)

What, then, is the significance of the prayers of the saints in this vision of the slain and resurrected Christ, who is the only one worthy to reveal the kingdom of God? These prayers accompany the new song of praise sung by the four living creatures and the twenty-four elders. The intensity of this praise mounts as it is joined first by the voices of myriads of angels (vv. 11–12), and then by every creature in creation (vv. 13–14). The Lamb then proceeds to open the seals one by one (6:1–17), and each is followed by a manifestation of judgment.[24] After the sixth seal John sees a vision of those redeemed out of Israel and from all the nations of the world (7:1–17). The breaking of the seventh seal leads us into a new group of visions of seven angels who blow the seven trumpets (8:1 – 11:19). But, before the trumpets are blown, the breaking of the seventh seal leads first to a brief intrusive vision in which another angel offers incense with the prayers of the saints.

The prayers of the saints, then, act as a kind of thematic bracket for the seals. And since the seventh seal reveals the seven trumpets

---

23. This is indicated in the following chapters as the seals are opened.
24. The opening of the fifth seal reveals the souls of the martyrs who cry out for judgment (vv. 9–11).

that, in turn, lead on to a further series of visions, we can say that the prayers are seen as a heavenly accompaniment of the judging work of God as he brings in his kingdom. In our examination of the Psalms we saw how the new song in Psalms 96 and 98 included a summons to rejoice because God comes to judge the world. We were reminded from our consideration of the Lord's Prayer and the petition 'Your kingdom come!' that this relationship of salvation and judgment is an all-pervasive biblical theme. In the same way, the thrust of the visions in Revelation is that salvation and the coming of God's kingdom are an aspect of his judgment. This anticipation of our final and full salvation, accompanied by the just judgment on all rebellion against God's kingdom, is the heart of biblical eschatology and the focus of our certain hope. Salvation and judgment are the work of our all-powerful God from beginning to end. Great biblical themes such as the eternal decrees of God, predestination, the new creation in Christ, the sufficiency of Christ's saving work, the sovereign working of the Holy Spirit, and the grace of perseverance all point to the fact that we are totally helpless to save ourselves or to contribute to the redemption of the universe. Yet here are the prayers of the saints at centre stage as the kingdom of God is revealed and as the judgments of God lead inexorably to the consummation of his purposes in the new heavens and the new earth. God's sovereign work of salvation achieves its goal *along with* the prayers of the saints. As we saw in chapter 4, God's purposes are carried out sovereignly as he gathers his people into a conscious sharing of what is revealed of those purposes. As we identify with the revealed will of God in prayer, we fulfil the Father's will for us to share in fellowship with him through his Son, a fellowship that is oriented to the future consummation of the Father's sovereign will.

Consideration of prayer in the book of Revelation would not be complete without some reference to the many hymns of praise to God that are included in John's visions.[25] The hymns are sung by a

---

25. I have discussed at greater length something of the function of the hymns in Revelation in *The Gospel in Revelation*, chapter 7, which is now included in *The Goldsworthy Trilogy* (Carlisle: Paternoster, 2000). The main hymnic passages are Rev. 4:8, 11; 5:9–10, 12, 13; 7:10, 12; 11:15, 17–18; 15:3–4; 16:5–7; 19:1–8.

variety of voices: the four living creatures, the twenty-four elders, angels, the saints of God, and a combination of every living creature in all creation. The contents include the following:

- Praise of the holiness of God (4:8).
- The worthiness of God as creator to receive all glory, honour and power (4:11).
- The new song praising the Lamb's worthiness to open the scroll because of his saving work (5:9–10, 12, 13).
- Praise offered by the nations for the salvation that belongs to God and the Lamb (7:10).
- Ascription of all honour and glory to God (7:12).
- The proclamation that the reign of Christ has come (11:15).
- Thanksgiving to God that he has taken his power to reign, and for the beginning of judgment (11:17–18).
- Praise of God for his marvellous deeds and the revealing of his judgment (15:3–4).
- The angel's praise of the judgments of God (16:5–7).
- Praise for God's judgments (19:1–5).
- Praise for the reign of God and for the coming of the marriage of the Lamb (19:6–8).

Although these hymns come in a variety of contexts and from a variety of sources, the common features are easily seen. They celebrate the glory of God and of the Lamb as it is revealed in the salvation that has been wrought. They praise the gospel of Christ which, as we have seen, is both a work of redemption of the people of God and a manifestation of judgment on all rebellion against God's kingdom. Bearing in mind that the book of Revelation as a whole was addressed to the suffering churches in Asia Minor, these hymns encapsulate the overall message of the book that is for the encouragement of the faithful who wait for the appearing of the Lord in glory. They emphasize that we have entered the last days with the earthly ministry, death and resurrection of Jesus.[26] John

26. See my discussion of this in *The Gospel in Revelation*, now included in *The Goldsworthy Trilogy* (Carlisle: Paternoster, 2000).

shares with them in the tribulation and the kingdom but encourages them with the message of the certainty of the outcome. As with the prayers of the saints brought before God, so with the praises; all demonstrate the eschatological orientation of all authentic prayer. We pray ever and only towards the consummation of the gospel.

Prayer and the knowledge of God

As we seek to sum up the emphases in the various aspects of prayer in the New Testament we are led to conclude that the revelation of God in his Son as the Word come in the flesh governs the authentic expression of our fellowship with the Father in prayer. In the Acts of the Apostles we noted the element of transition from the time of Jesus' ministry in the flesh to his ministry through his Spirit and the preaching of the gospel. Difficulties arose because the apostles and other disciples were at times slow to adjust to the new dispensation of the Spirit and the fulfilment of the long-since revealed purposes of God. By contrast, the letters of Paul show a mature understanding of the implications of Jesus as the fulfiller of all the hopes and expectations of the Old Testament. He is clear that the believers know God and he prays that they will grow in that knowledge. His reported prayers indicate that he desires that the gospel will have its full outworking in their lives and in their fellowship with him in the ministry of the gospel. The general epistles share this outlook. Hebrews, as we have seen, takes us to great heights in understanding the ministry of the risen Christ in terms of fulfilling the Old Testament ministries. The book of Revelation takes us both upwards and forward. Prayer is seen in its heavenly and eschatological context as we are shown how the gospel events, and the present sufferings of the churches, find their consummation in the new heavens and the new earth.

Summary

- The dimensions of prayer in the Old Testament are now fulfilled in the earthly ministry of Jesus.
- There is a transition from the Old Testament content of prayer to its

fulfilment based on the final revelation of God in Christ. Jesus is shown to be the teacher of prayer, and to give the perfect human response in prayer to the knowledge of God.

- Acts shows the difficult adjustment of the disciples to the reality of the ascended Christ and the fulfilment of the Old Testament promises.
- The epistles exemplify the full transformation of perspective from Old Testament covenant and eschatology to the realization of these in Christ.
- Revelation points to the consummation and how prayer is related to it. Petition for the reaching of the end is transformed into praise for the glory that is fully revealed.

Pause a moment . . .

Consider the implications for our prayers of the finished work of Christ. When you contemplate God bringing about his purposes, do you mainly think about:

- a remote future event, or
- what God has done, is doing, and will do?

Think again about the goodness and love of the Father who allows us to share, through prayer, in the achieving of the goals of his sovereign will. Are you learning to think God's thoughts after him?

11 Conclusion – 'What do you think about the Christ?'

In retrospect

In beginning our study with Jesus as he reveals God, and in understanding something of the implications of this God being Trinity, we have been able to place the subject of prayer in its fuller context of the sovereign will and purpose of God. We have thus, hopefully, avoided the worst excesses of a human-centred approach that works in opposition to revelation. We can now summarize the main features of our study which, I hope, will make the subject of prayer more intelligible and provide the proper foundation for any Christian to develop his or her own particular practice of prayer. Practice must remain largely an individual and personal matter, while being kept in the bounds of freedom provided by the character of God and the nature of our relationship with him. It is also a collective concern as we consider the function of prayer in the congregation or fellowship group.

It should be obvious that prayer is a major experiential aspect of our relationship with God. By experiential I mean our experience as it involves our self-conscious being as believers, that is, our thinking and our practice. It will impinge upon our wills and emotions. While experience is something that is individual, subjective and human, it is of necessity interpreted by principles revealed in the word of God that are general, objective and divine. Every prayer offered in the name of Jesus or 'through Jesus Christ our Lord' is an acknowledgment that prayer depends on our relationship to God as redeemed children adopted by grace. Calvin's understanding of prayer as the chief expression of our faith is important. It links prayer indissolubly with Christology, since faith, as we have seen, is defined by its object, namely Christ. The object of faith is Jesus our Lord, the crucified and risen Saviour. What has emerged in this study is that prayer is a function of who and what we perceive Christ to be, and of how we understand our relationship to God the Father through Christ's mediation. Pastorally speaking, when we are confronted by someone who finds all kinds of difficulties with prayer, theoretical, theological or practical, we need to treat this first of all as a matter of faith. It may be rather oblique to ask, 'What do you think about the Christ? Whose son is he?'[1] Yet, in effect, that is exactly where we need to go, however we achieve it. To put it another way: just as practical questions about faith need to be dealt with, not by focusing primarily on individuals and the strength or weakness of their faith, but on God revealed in Jesus as the object of faith, so it is with prayer.

The link between prayer and faith is so firm that questions about prayer are inevitably questions about faith and must be dealt with as such. A person with no real concern for who and what Christ is will distort the notion of prayer. Thus unbelievers who shoot the occasional panic-call straight towards 'the Man upstairs' know nothing of the mediatorial role of Jesus and in reality pray to gods of their own imagining. The Christian whose prayer life is stunted by a fixation on 'dear Jesus' prayers has also lost sight of the Father who has sent his Son to be the mediator between him and us. This is, of course, not as serious an error as that committed by those who divert their prayers to other supposed mediators such as Mary or one of the saints. But it is similar in this regard, that God the Father wants us to address him through the mediation of his Son. If we pray only to 'dear Jesus' then we have not understood who he is and why he came. It may seem frivolous to point out that Jesus did not pray to himself, but it is not a

1. Matt. 22:42.

meaningless observation. We worship the risen and ascended Christ as the Lord God, but we worship him truly as the Son of the Father, and as the mediator who brings us into fellowship with his Father. The ascended Christ, even now, intercedes for us with the Father. Once again we face the difficulty that finite humans have in responding to the revealed nature of God as Trinity.

I believe that a lot that is said and written about prayer tackles the problems from the wrong end. Unfortunately many Christians are imbued with the spirit of our age and want the quick fix. The culture of fast food and instant everything permeates our thinking when dealing with problems. But it is well said that when all else fails we should read the maker's handbook of instructions. The purely problem-oriented approach to prayer that tackles it from the human and phenomenological perspective is not at all promising. I am not suggesting that we should never 'scratch where people itch', or that we should ignore the perceived problems that people may have with regard to prayer, but we need to go beyond the perceived problems to address the real issue beneath them. The spiritual shot in the arm that many get from convention talks or sermons will often cause them to give rave reviews about the speaker and to exclaim how 'helpful' the studies have been. We easily give in to quite subjective criteria for judging the worth of an exposition. The real criterion for the judgment of worth is Scripture.

It is not to be wondered at that legalism is seen so often to be helpful in issues of Christian living. This is because it focuses on the rules for doing, and we prefer that to the responsibility of searching out the biblical principles that apply. At the same time that we are extolling the benefits of such practical teaching, we are probably reverting to type, succumbing to the same problems, and longing for the next talk on reviving our prayer life. Good practice, however, requires a good understanding of what it is we are practising. Far better that we try to understand what the Bible is teaching us about the nature of prayer and how it is intended to function. Far, far better that we spend some time thinking about the theology of prayer, the implications of Christology for prayer, and what it means to pray in the Spirit before worrying about the practicalities of our own prayer lives. As with most things, sound practice involves a sound theoretical basis, that is, the theological principles revealed in Scripture.

An English missionary doctor, who had suffered imprisonment at the hands of the revolutionary powers in Iran, was subsequently released and returned home. After telling something of his harrowing experiences at a meeting, a person confronted him and said, 'I wish I had your faith.' His reply was wise and revealing: 'You don't need my faith; you need my Lord.'[2] The link between faith in Christ and prayer justifies the adaptation of this theologically perceptive reply to the subject of prayer. A Christian might conceivably remark to a speaker who has expounded the subject of prayer, 'I wish I had your ability to pray.' An appropriate reply would be: 'You don't need my ability to pray; you need my Lord.' I hasten to add that a pastorally sensitive approach might require us to be a little less direct but, nevertheless, to help this person to see that the way we pray should reflect the way we understand Christ as Lord and Saviour, and the way we come to him in our thinking and doing. In short, it should reflect our knowledge of God. The question, 'What do you think of Christ?', could well be indirectly approached by asking the seemingly innocuous question, 'How do you pray?'

Reaffirming the principles

The basic principles of prayer can now be summarized:

- The reality of prayer is found in the discoursing Trinity before ever there were people to pray to this God. That Father, Son and Holy Spirit have communicated from all eternity is now reflected in our being created in God's image as speaking, communicating beings. One aspect of sin is that human beings have cut God out of their conversational circle. Insofar as prayer comes into our thinking, it is made to idols.
- The basis of our prayer is the Sonship of Jesus that we share in when

2. Recounted by this missionary, Dr John Coleman, in a sermon at St Stephen's Anglican Church, Brisbane, at some time in the 1980s. It echoes the statement of the great missionary Hudson Taylor that we don't need great faith in God, so much as faith in a great God.

we are united to him by faith. That Jesus could address the Father and be heard means that we also, in Christ, can address the Father and be heard.

- The source of prayer is the Fatherhood of God, who works all things according to his sovereign will and who allows us to share in the outworking of his revealed saving purposes through our prayer.
- The enabling of prayer is the indwelling of the Holy Spirit, who gives to God's elect people the grace to believe in Jesus Christ as Saviour and Lord, to understand and receive the revelation of God in his word, and to call upon him in believing prayer according to that revelation.
- The progress of prayer in the Bible displays a clear emphasis on prayer as a grace of the covenant relationship of God to his people. In the Old Testament it is primarily displayed in the covenant functionaries whose ministries are meaningful only because they foreshadow the ministry of Christ as prophet, priest, king and wise man.
- The mediation of prayer in the Old Testament is fulfilled in the New Testament by the prayer of Jesus as the acceptable Son of God. This unbreakable link between prayer and Jesus Christ means that all authentic prayer is prayer towards the fulfilling of God's purposes in the gospel.
- All prayer in the New Testament is prayer to the Father, through the Son, enabled by the power of the Holy Spirit.[3] The unity of the persons of the Trinity means that in praying to any one person, we are praying to all three. The distinctions between the persons mean that we should maintain the biblical perspective on the distinct roles of each in our prayer, that is, prayer is *essentially* to the Father, through the Son, and enabled by the Spirit.

Knowing God and having fellowship with him

In stressing the importance of the knowledge of God I have raised the issue of how that knowledge can be achieved and what it means.

3. With the three exceptions noted in chapter 10.

In essence we have seen how a biblical-theological survey of the unfolding revelation in the Bible indicates some vital aspects of what it means to know God. The history of the human race begins with its creation in the image of God and with the ability to know God through the evidence in creation and by the word especially spoken to humankind. Paul's assessment (Rom. 1:18–32) of the effect of the human rebellion against the word of the Lord, narrated in Genesis 3, is that the human race has suppressed the truth in wickedness. Yet there is still some vestige of the image so that, as Calvin puts it, we have within us a sense of deity.[4] The suppression of the truth that is within and around us leaves us without excuse for our rebellion. The fellowship of mankind with God, as experienced in Eden, is lost as Adam and Eve are cast out of the garden. The human condition is subsequently one of rebellious defiance of God, and a complete repudiation of both the just Lordship of God and of our fellowship with him. Universal religiosity and the common human aspiration for life after death are turned aside into religious ideas and practices that serve as idolatrous diversions from the truth. Of this condition, Paul can say that,

> None is righteous, no, not one;
> no one understands;
> no one seeks for God.
>
> (Rom. 3:10–11)

We followed the progress of prayer along with the progress of God's revelation of himself in his covenantal and redemptive purposes. These purposes, established from all eternity, were put in motion from the moment of the fall and the judicial removal of humans from the presence and fellowship of God. Grace is revealed as the undeserved attention of God to a race that deserves only to be completely cut off. The biblical genealogy of Adam through Seth shows a line of people under the merciful care of God. It is from within this line that people begin to call upon the name of the Lord. This points implicitly to the relationship of prayer to the covenant

4. John Calvin, *Institutes of the Christian Religion*, Book I, chapter 3.

grace of God. The covenant relationship is made more explicit with Noah, and then even more so with Abraham. It is clear that God takes the initiative and exercises his sovereignty in graciously enabling an elect people to become his friends and to know him. We do not need to rehearse again the material of our biblical-theological survey. We have observed the relationship between prayer and the knowledge of God. We have also seen that knowledge of God is a great deal more that knowing things about God. God not only reveals the truth about himself in the outworking of redemption, but he also comes to his people and makes himself present among them. We must emphatically repudiate and reject the dichotomy between knowing about God and knowing him as a person who comes to us. The God who comes to us and who allows us to know him and to be his friends is the God of redemptive history. He is the holy and undivided Trinity. He is the God and Father of our Lord Jesus Christ. He is, above all, the God whom we can only truly know when we are restored to fellowship with him through faith in his Son our Saviour. In short, we cannot know God without at the same time knowing the truth about him. That is how God's plan and purpose for his people works.

Prayer and the knowledge of God

Prayer, then, is the result of knowing God. It is inseparable from both knowing the truth that God reveals about himself in his word *and* knowing him as the God who saves us and makes himself present to us. Prayer is a primary means by which God, who is the source of all personhood, allows us to interact with him on a personal basis. We need to go beyond using the idea of a personal relationship with God as a cliché that is undefined and undefinable. The knowledge of God impinges upon us as persons and affects the way we think, act and feel. The essence of this knowledge is that we know the Father as the Father of the Son, Jesus Christ. It is important to grasp that, while this personal relationship of fellowship with God will have a variety of effects on our emotions and feelings, the reality of our fellowship is not dependent upon these. We may from time to time feel subjectively that we are rather out of touch with God. This could be the result of a rebelliousness of spirit on our part as we entertain some sinful desires or behaviour that we know full well to be displeasing to God. At other times it may be due to being ill or depressed, or to some intangible cause. At such times it is important to realize that our fellowship with God and his presence with us is a function of the fellowship of Jesus with the Father. Fellowship with God, and the prayer it generates, is thus first and foremost a function of our union with Christ by faith.

Another name for the knowledge of God is theology. Unfortunately many regard theology as an exercise in abstractions for intellectuals. This may be a reaction against some forms of academic theology that, we have to admit, have often largely lost their way and ceased to be biblical and are therefore not a way to knowledge of God. It is also to be regretted that the teaching of sound doctrine in churches is all too rare in this day and age. Yet the fact remains that every Christian is a theologian in that every Christian knows God and, hopefully, strives to know him better. The question is not whether we are or are not theologians, but how well we want to know God. It is a matter of what kind of theologians we want to be. In this study I have attempted to bring the most practical matter of prayer together with the most basic theological matter: the knowledge of God. In doing so I have had recourse to both systematic theology (Christian doctrine) and biblical theology (theology as it is revealed progressively in the biblical documents). I hope I have thereby whetted the reader's appetite for a more concerted study of both these disciplines.

Characteristics of authentic prayer

On the basis of our knowledge of God from the revelation of Scripture, we can sum up the characteristics of authentic Christian prayer in a series of propositions. These can provide a theological underpinning for the development of our personal and congregational practice of prayer. On reflection we may conclude that we have been almost instinctively guided by most of these principles as we seek to pray in a manner consistent with our desire to be biblical in faith and practice. In this case, I trust that reflection upon these dimensions and their biblical underpinning would deepen our desire to pray and our understanding of what is happening when we do pray. But it may also be the case that this fairly analytical approach will act as an incentive for us to strive for reform where it is needed.

Prayer is always trinitarian

When I hear people, often church-goers, talk only in terms of 'faith in God', I wonder about their understanding of the unique role of Jesus Christ as Saviour and Lord. When prayer is only addressed to a 'Thou' who seems to remain without specific identity, again I become uneasy about the knowledge of God, or lack of it, being expressed by the person praying. When prayer is consistently finished with 'Amen' but without any reference to the mediation of Jesus, I sense that those praying have no real understanding of the mediatorial role of Jesus. Our examination of the biblical evidence brings us to conclude that prayer must be trinitarian in nature. This does not mean that the mere use of certain trinitarian formulas makes our prayer authentic. It does mean that faith expressed in prayer is only faith insofar as it is faith in the God of the Bible: Father, Son and Holy Spirit. Thus we recognize the following:

- Prayer is a gift of God the Father and is grounded in the revelation of his will for us.
- Prayer is only possible when it is mediated by the Son with whom we are united by faith. Faith is thus defined by its object, namely Jesus, in his saving life, death and resurrection.
- Prayer is only possible when the Holy Spirit of God regenerates us and turns us to the Son in trust and faith so that we might have fellowship with the Father.

Prayer is always Christological

This does not mean that we always need to utter the name Jesus with our prayer as a kind of password to gain access to God. It does mean, however, that authentic prayer can only be offered in the confidence that it is solely through faith in Jesus' living and dying for us. It is Christological in the sense that it is shaped by the conviction that we approach our heavenly Father as the God who has sent his Son to be our substitute and representative. It is Christological in that it is shaped by what God has revealed through Christ of his eternal purpose for the world and us. It is Christological because Christian prayer is offered on the basis of our union with Christ. One thing that truly Christological prayer emphatically does not mean is that it is prayer only to Christ.[5] It does mean that we acknowledge the role of Jesus Christ as the one mediator between God and man (1 Tim. 2:5). It means that Christ-centred prayer is centred on the biblical Christ who gives us access to the Father. It can only be truly Christ-centred if it is also God-centred.

Prayer is always predestinarian

I do not mean by this that only those who are totally committed Calvinists and believe implicitly in the Reformation doctrine of predestination can pray.[6] I do mean that Christian prayer, being grounded in faith in Christ, is an acknowledgment of the truth, stated by Paul in Romans 8:29, that God has predestined us to be conformed to the image of his Son. Every petition that we make to God, if it is truly grounded in the revealed will of God for us, will presuppose that the granting of such a petition can serve only as a means to this end. Prayer is predestinarian in that it acknowledges that the source of prayer is the sovereign will of God, that the motive for prayer is the action of God, and that the enabler of prayer is the Spirit of God. As we recognize prayer as one aspect of letting our salvation have its outworking in our lives, we will also know that it is God who is at work in us both to will and to do his good pleasure (Phil. 2:12–13). Prayer is predestinarian in that it involves, not our bending of God's will to ours, but his conforming of our will to his. Prayer is predestinarian in that it expresses confidence in a God who

5. A focus on Christ to the exclusion of the legitimate focus on God the Father is an error that is sometimes reflected in neo-orthodoxy. Such 'Christomonism' is also implicit in some forms of piety that do not reflect the orthodox understanding of the Trinity.
6. Statements of this doctrine can be found in *The Thirty-nine Articles of Religion* (Anglican), article XVII; *The Westminster Confession of Faith* (Presbyterian), chapter III; *The Canons of Dort* (Reformed), First Head of Doctrine: Divine Election and Reprobation.

works all things according to his will, who can and will achieve his purposes.

Prayer is always eschatological

I have, I think, shown enough biblical evidence for us to be able to declare that prayer is always directed towards the biblical goals that God has revealed. It is not only predestinarian, for many a somewhat deterministic idea,[7] but it is eschatological, which is a teleological notion involving purpose. This means that it partakes in a purpose of reaching a defined goal or end. Biblically speaking, of course, predestination is never mere determinism. It tells us that God has a specific goal, namely the bringing of many sons and daughters to glory. The eschatology of the Bible, as it is progressively revealed in the unfolding drama of redemption, contrasts with the status quo aims of both ancient and modern paganism.[8] The whole linear notion of history in the Bible contrasts with the pagan concept of cyclic history. The details of our lives can never be conceived of as merely the means of maintaining a stable life-situation. If we pray for health, safety or our daily bread, it is in order to be able to live another day to serve God and to share in the outworking of his purposes.

Prayer is always covenantal

If God had not created the world in covenant relationship with himself, and made a specific covenant with his people, prayer would be impossible. In this covenant relationship there is established a

---

7. Deterministic in the sense of denying any personal purposiveness that is directed towards some goal. The misunderstanding that the doctrine of predestination makes us like puppets on a string comes from such a deterministic view of the matter.
8. G. E. Wright, *God Who Acts: Biblical Theology as Recital*, Studies in Biblical Theology, No. 8 (London: SCM, 1952). The idea of the polytheistic or pagan status quo is that religion maintains the present order of things. Status quo means an unchanging position. For the ancient Canaanites this meant that the whole of its religion was meant to ensure a cycle of prosperity that followed the cycle of the seasons of the year. Israel, by contrast, had a linear view of history leading to the *eschaton* ordained by God.

bond of friendship and fellowship, which, from God's side, is never repudiated. The unity of the various covenantal expressions lies in their being the formal means of conveying, through grace alone, the title to the kingdom of God to the people of God. The nature of the biblical covenant, then, is such that we also see that prayer is grounded in grace alone. We have seen how the Christology of the gospel, especially the fact that Jesus is both true God and true man, points us to the nature of the relationships within the Trinity, and the relationship of God's sovereignty to our human responsibility. The covenantal nature of prayer means that it expresses such a divine–human relationship. Without God's election and calling we have no basis of communication with him. Without his sovereign grace acting through the Holy Spirit to give us new birth and to create in us true saving faith, there could be no prayer. Yet prayer is a truly human response to the divine revelation and action. But placing us and our prayer into a covenantal relationship with him, God binds us to hear and obey him. He also binds himself to us to hear us and to respond in accordance with his holy character. That the covenant is a covenant of grace is shown in the fact that God binds himself in covenant faithfulness to his elect, to provide for them the righteousness and justification that they cannot provide for themselves.

Prayer is always a reflection of our knowledge of God

This is the unavoidable conclusion of our investigation. Our knowledge of God is the only basis of our knowledge of ourselves as created in the image of God. It is the only basis for our understanding of what our rebellion against God means, and what effect it has on us. It is the only basis for our understanding of what it is to be justified by faith and restored to fellowship with God. It is the basis for our understanding of what the gift of prayer really is and on what basis it exists. And our knowledge of God is the only basis for a true understanding of the world around us. Without such knowledge of God we could not know the reality of prayer or its nature. We could not know if there were anyone to hear us, nor what response would be forthcoming if our prayer were to be heard. Without knowledge of God we could utter only self-centred prayers to a god or gods who may or may not be there, and who may or may not have the will or the power to respond in any meaningful way. Without knowledge of

God we might pray for ourselves and others to be saved from a meaningless death and from non-existence after death, but we could not really know if we have anything but extinction to look forward to. We could not know if we were in touch with reality or merely engaging in fantasy with as much substance as a fairy tale. Only knowledge of the God of the Bible can assure us that our lives have both meaning and an eternal destiny. Only such assurance can make prayer a meaningful part of our daily lives.

Coming back to practicalities

To bring this study to a close I want to focus on some practical issues that arise from time to time and that need to be addressed carefully in the light of biblical teaching. It is important that we always acknowledge that theology or biblical study is not done for its own sake. It is done that God's glory might be better understood and proclaimed. It is done that we might be conformed more and more to the image of Christ, to the glory of God the Father. We may not perceive the immediate practical implications, but we should always be mindful of the fact that the theologian and the biblical scholar should aim to serve the people of God. The following, then, are some of the issues that come to mind as we consider the theological underpinning of the practice of prayer.

Practicalities can never be allowed to be pragmatic

Pragmatism is the name given to a philosophical position that holds to the primacy of usefulness. If something works then it must be good. If a theory appears to work, it must be true. In Christian practice it is sometimes expressed as, 'If the Lord is blessing what we are doing, we must be doing the right thing.' This, of course, raises other issues that we cannot go into here, such as how we identify the Lord's blessing. The problem with pragmatism is that it is essentially a human-centred approach. I am not suggesting that Christian pragmatists do not believe that God is at work, but the assessment of what is or is not a work or blessing of God is often opportunistic. What pastor or church, for example, does not want to be seen to be successful? So, if the people are coming in increasing numbers, we must be doing it right and the Lord is blessing us. The tactics used are thus not questioned. Yet numbers in themselves indicate neither faithfulness nor unfaithfulness. A big congregation is not necessarily a congregation of the faithful, nor is it necessarily a congregation of people who are growing to a mature understanding of God's word. Only biblical standards can indicate what is true blessing. Thus, a particularly superficial evangelistic sermon without any real substance or gospel content may be followed by an appeal that leads to several people responding to the 'altar call'. There is general rejoicing and we assume we must be doing it right. But are we? So we pray that the preacher will go on as before and that the Lord will bring many more to faith. Given that many conversions are the result of a whole string of events involving different people's input, it is fatuous to suppose that any genuine conversions were solely the result of the prayer and the preacher's style of preaching. Both prayer and preaching must be subject to constant testing by the standards of Scripture. God is so good that he sometimes seems to use us even in spite of ourselves, but that does not justify our neglect of Scripture.

Praying without ceasing

Paul's injunction in 1 Thessalonians 5:17 cannot possibly mean that life is to be one constant prayer twenty-four hours of every day. For a start, in the same sentence he exhorts us to 'Rejoice always, pray without ceasing, give thanks in all circumstances; for this is the will of God in Christ Jesus for you.' Clearly we cannot do all this in a literal sense. Equally clearly, Paul intends us to understand that rejoicing, prayer and thanksgiving are to be permanent characteristics of living as a Christian. Although it may be a contentious issue for some, I cannot see that having an all-night marathon of prayer is necessarily any more effective that a more conventional meeting. Neither would I suggest that it is wrong to arrange an all-night prayer vigil on occasions. The issue is not how long we pray but how constantly, and how consistently with Scripture. There is, of course, a mystery here that defies quantification, either in time spent or numbers of praying people involved. If this investigation has shown anything it is that time spent and the numbers who spend it, if they seem to correlate with blessings received, are not a matter of our impressing God, but of his involving us as willing co-operators in the outworking of his will.

Avoiding legalism while exercising self-discipline

Most of us need some kind of self-discipline in all kinds of things that we do on a regular basis. Usually we don't have any difficulty in having three meals a day, but some do. We get into a routine for eating, sleeping and going to work. One routine that is often observed is the 'quiet time', particularly by Christians who recognize the need to study the Bible and to pray, usually on a daily basis. A quiet time is a good routine, but it needs to have some flexibility. The quiet time can become a legalistic requirement to the point that some feel that if they sleep in and have to miss their quiet time, their whole day will be a virtual disaster. This borders on superstition. The person who cultivates the art of praying without ceasing will recognize that, like the Sabbath, the quiet time was made for man and not man for the quiet time! All kinds of things can interrupt our routines, from storm, tempest, flood, fire and earthquakes. Or it may be simply a neighbour in need who calls on us, or a sick child. On the other hand, the person who makes a habit of chaotic indiscipline needs to take this matter in hand. However we might discipline our day to include Bible-reading and prayer, it is important not to reduce this habit to the level of the fulfilment of a legal obligation. It is always a privilege for the children of God and, as such, it is an expression of our being saved by grace alone.

Teaching the children to pray and praying for the children

Christian parents have a vital ministry in the church. The Christian nurture of children is primarily the responsibility of the parents, not the day school (even if it is a Christian school) nor the Sunday school. Unfortunately, in our modern society, mothers who stay at home to care for their children are often considered to be unemployed and to have sold out on the right of women to pursue a career. There can be no nobler career than nurturing Christian children to be well-adjusted citizens of our society and to be faithful citizens of the kingdom of God.[9] At the heart of this ministry is the role of both

9. I imply no criticism of the many Christian mothers who do work, who choose to should do so for the right reasons and not simply to be able to afford a more affluent lifestyle. My concern here is the secular pressure on those who

parents (and grandparents if there are any) to pray that the children will grow to be strong in faith and good works for the Lord. In a Christian home the children will be taught the stories of Jesus and about the mighty acts of God. They will be taught about the love that God has shown us in sending Jesus to die for us and to be our friend. They will be taught to pray and, hopefully, taught to pray in a biblical fashion. That is why the common practice of teaching children only 'Dear Lord Jesus' prayers needs some rethinking. Of course it is true that younger children can grasp more easily the concept of Jesus as a man here on earth than the notion of the Trinity. Perhaps we need to concentrate more on teaching children that one of the things Jesus has done for us is to make us friends with his Father in heaven so that we can talk to him and call him Father. Children will most readily learn the 'art' of praying by listening to their parents or other adults praying. It is therefore important for us to be consciously modelling a biblical mode of prayer for our children.

Prayer in church

A lot depends on what we think doing church is all about. Some Christians see the special building to be all-important for our relationship with God. For them there is a particular sanctity to the building, or to a certain focal point within it, that it makes prayer in a church building somehow more efficacious. I cannot see any support for this notion in the New Testament. The matter is not helped by the practice of referring to the building, or one part of it, as the sanctuary, as if it fulfilled the biblical role. The sanctuary is an Old Testament term and is used particularly with regard to the temple in Jerusalem. But the New Testament writers recognize Jesus as the new temple, and that the presence of the Spirit constitutes our bodies as his temple. Beyond that, there is also the heavenly temple that Hebrews deals with. A church building is not a biblical notion, and church buildings certainly do not function as new temples. Church buildings are thus convenient meeting places for the church, the congregation of the faithful, and have no inherent sanctity.

---

believe that it is their God-given calling to stay at home with their children to conform to the modern pattern of working mothers.

Prayer, as with the worship of God, does not take place in holy places but in Spirit and in truth (John 4:21–24). To go into a church building to pray is sometimes convenient, particularly for city workers, in that one can stand, sit or kneel in relative quietness and pray without interruption.

But what of the prayer offered within a church meeting or service? While there is a great range of possibilities for the nature of such gatherings, the same principles surely apply as in the matter of personal and private prayer. In the context of a congregation, the focus will usually be on the more general interests of the group, but the nature of the prayer will be the same. Some traditions of a liturgical or 'set' form of service are structured on the various dimensions of a Christian's life before God. The order may vary, but the ingredients expressed in prayer will include confession of sins, thanksgiving for forgiveness through Christ, praise, petition and general thanksgiving. The petitionary prayers may reflect the common concerns for sick and suffering people, for the secular state and its leaders, for the church and/or denomination, for mission, and for the coming of the kingdom of God.

The language of prayer

There is now a common forsaking of the Elizabethan English that once found general acceptance because of the influence of the King James Version of the Bible. Few people, in extemporary prayer, would use the 'thee' and 'thou' addresses, or perpetuate the archaic verb forms of the second person.[10] Even liturgical revisions have mostly changed to use modern English expressions. The abandonment of a special language for praying is on the whole seen as a good thing; the down-side is the disrespectful vernacular that is sometimes used in extemporary prayers. This is a matter of opinion and touches on questions of both appealing to the unchurched or the ordinary person, and showing respect and reverence towards God. In theological terms it shows a tension between trying to express something of God's condescension and immanence (his being 'down here with us') while preserving a sense of his transcendence (his being 'out there

10. Such as 'thou wouldest' or 'thou goest'.

and beyond us'). It is a matter of communicating relevance with reverence. The idiom we use may not be the most important issue. In the light of this study, surely we have to say that our main concern should be how we address God, and what kind of prayers we direct to him. How we address him includes the names of God that we use. These are clear from the Bible and it is not an option, in the interests of inclusive language, to address God as Mother, or to refer to the Holy Spirit as She. Nor is it an option to constantly substitute vaguely, or even specifically, modalistic titles for the ontological names of the Trinity. Thus, only to address God as Creator, Redeemer and Sanctifier is to replace the self-revealed name of God with certain functions. God has given us his names by which he is identified as the God of the Bible, the God and Father of our Lord Jesus Christ.[11]

Read prayers: dead prayers?

Much depends on the tradition of one's ecclesiastical upbringing and preferences when it comes to assessing the relative advantages or disadvantages of set liturgical forms of prayer. Having been nurtured in the Anglican liturgical tradition since my conversion at sixteen years of age, I found myself from time to time having to defend it against the retort that 'read prayers are dead prayers'. During my many years spent in this liturgical fold, great changes have taken place. There have been significant liturgical revisions away from the Elizabethan English of the 1662 *Book of Common Prayer* in most parts of the Anglican Communion.[12] From a biblical point of view, some of the revisions show the regrettable influence of various forms of theological modernism. However, one advantage of most of the revisions is that they are usually characterized by the provision of a greater

---

11. Alvin F. Kimel comments, 'The Holy Trinity is the God who has named himself Father, Son, and Holy Spirit. To abandon or reject the trinitarian naming is to create a new religion, a new God.' See Kimel, 'The God Who Likes His Name: Holy Trinity, Feminism, and the Language of Faith', *Interpretation* 45/2 (1991).
12. The Anglican Communion amounts to a loose co-operative fellowship of autonomous Anglican Churches that are mostly organized on national bases.

variety of choice so that familiarity and predictability can be largely avoided. A common feature in many Anglican churches, as with those of other denominations, is a variety of Sunday Services including, usually in the evening, a relatively non-liturgical gathering featuring more modern music. In assessing the relative virtues of liturgical versus non-liturgical prayer, I have come to conclude the following:

- Both liturgical (set, read prayers) and non-liturgical (extemporized) prayers can be dead and formalistic, but neither of them need be.
- Non-liturgical services can be as predictable as liturgical services, and often are. The prayers can be just as lacking in spontaneity as liturgical prayers.
- It is simply a fact that some people respond better to set prayers, while others find them almost intolerable. It is a personal matter, sometimes of temperament, sometimes of habit.
- The advantage of extemporary prayer is that it can be more open to the spontaneous movement of the Spirit of God.
- The disadvantage of extemporary prayer is that the person praying may express quite theologically unsound sentiments, or give way to sentimentality or to shear verbosity.
- The advantage of liturgical prayer is that it is usually concise and to the point and, in the case of the *Book of Common Prayer*, biblically and theologically sound.[13] Later revisions have tended to be less theologically consistent.
- The disadvantage of liturgical prayer is that it can encourage formalism and stifle any spontaneity. It can lack variety and applicability to many modern situations.
- We can only suppose that Jesus and the apostles were brought up with a fair measure of liturgy in the Jewish traditions. Yet, there are

13. Again speaking from my knowledge of the Australian Anglican scene, Archbishop Cranmer's collects (set prayers for each Sunday) are taken from his Protestant Prayer Book of 1552, which provides the basis for the 1662 Restoration Prayer Book (after Cromwell's Commonwealth). The revision of 1978, *An Australian Prayer Book*, mostly translates Cranmer's collects into modern English, but also provides an alternative prayer in each case. These show much the same basic perspective on prayer as the older collects.

clearly spontaneous and extemporary prayers offered from time to time. There would seem to be room for both. What is important is that prayer, whether read or extemporized, should be biblical and reflect a true knowledge of God.

'Oh God, if there is a God . . .'

Sometimes it is suggested to unbelievers in an evangelistic context that they should pray that, if there is a God, he would reveal himself to the supplicant. This might seem to transgress all the principles that I have arrived at in this study. If, however, one suggests it to an agnostic, who is apparently unconvinced by apologetic argument that becoming a Christian is the only viable decision, it may have some justification. It has sometimes been proposed as a preliminary to reading the New Testament or part of it. In this case, a person who has had the gospel and the claims of Christ presented to them may well be coming under the gracious influence of the Spirit of God. The prayer may then be the first step in coming to see that the Scripture's witness to Christ is trustworthy. God is able to convert the most hardened atheist or agnostic, and the process of such conversion may conceivably include the use of such a prayer without this in any way becoming a normative way to pray. For the atheist the movement may well be from the firm conviction that no God exists, through the stage of agnosticism (God may exist but we can't know), to the stage of accepting that he might exist as the God revealed in Christ. Such a prayer could only be prayed as either a further expression of unbelief, or as the result of the Spirit's work as the person moves towards genuine faith. It is inconceivable as the prayer of one who has come to genuine faith.

Bruce Wilkinson's book, 'The prayer of Jabez'[14]

My only reason for commenting on a specific book is that it is, by all accounts, enjoying extraordinary success and influencing many

---

14. This refers to the book by Bruce Wilkinson, *The Prayer of Jabez* (Sisters: Multnomah, 2000). I am responding to a number of requests and suggestions that a book about prayer would be incomplete without comment on this modern publishing phenomenon.

people's thinking. It seems to have taken on a life of its own as a growth industry. It is reported to have been a number one bestseller in Christian bookstores and was also a number one New York Times bestseller.[15] It is critiqued in an article by Luke Tattersall (see note 15), and also in a satirical book by Douglas Jones.[16] This rejoinder by Jones, though written as a semi-humorous parody, deserves to be taken very seriously. The prayer that has so taken hold of Wilkinson's attention is found in 1 Chronicles 4:9–10:

> Jabez was more honorable than his brothers; and his mother called his name Jabez, saying, 'because I bore him in pain.' Jabez called upon the God of Israel, saying, 'Oh that you would bless me and enlarge my border, and that your hand might be with me, and that you would keep me from harm so that it might not bring me pain!' And God granted what he asked.

Two main criticisms spring to mind. First, *The Prayer of Jabez* argues from a totally pragmatic position. People are urged to pray this prayer of Jabez daily, and are promised remarkable results. It works, or has reportedly worked, for the author and others, therefore it must be a true interpretation of this snippet of biblical text. Secondly, and connected with the first point, is that such pragmatic interpretation is only possible by ignoring the biblical-theological context and by using the Bible as a kind of lucky-dip. The result is, as Tattersall so ably points out, that the real significance of the Old Testament passage in its relation to the fulfilment in Christ is ignored. The author has taken a brief reference from the Old Testament and turned it into a lifestyle. He has ignored the significance of the text in its own context, and has abandoned any effort to understand how this passage finds its fulfilment in Christ. There are many assertions that purport to be biblical but without justification from the Bible. In expanding the notion of territory in Jabez's prayer ('enlarge my

---

15. As reported in Luke Tattersall, 'The Prayer of Jabez and Other Misuses of the Bible', *The Briefing*, No. 281, Feb. 2002 (published by Matthias Media, Sydney).
16. Douglas M. Jones, *The Mantra of Jabez* (Moscow, Idaho: Canon Press, 2001).

border'), Wilkinson disregards any sense of its fulfilment in the person of Christ. Many of the items said to be derived from this aspect of the prayer are quite biblical, but are not related to the Old Testament theme of the promised land. The content of 'blessing' is assumed. The key to blessing is this prayer, rather than our access to every blessing that we possess in and through Christ (Eph. 1:3). Douglas Jones is correct in his assessment that Wilkinson's approach to 1 Chronicles 4:9–10 amounts to using a mantra in a way that expresses spiritual immaturity. It represents a perspective on prayer that is subjective, speculative and totally pragmatic. Much of what Wilkinson says is commendable, especially in urging Christians to pray for greater opportunities to proclaim the gospel and minister. But these are prayers that most Christians would pray on the basis of clear New Testament teaching, not as a spurious application of some supposed secret to great blessing. Praying a brief Old Testament prayer cannot be, as Wilkinson asserts, 'the key to a life of extraordinary favour with God'. Favour with God comes from sovereign grace and by means of the justification of the sinner through faith in Christ. We can never earn favour with God, since it is a gift of grace. Prayer, and particularly this prayer, is treated by Wilkinson as a meritorious work. Why this prayer and not any of the many others in Scripture is never explained.

Is meditation acceptable prayer?

The words meditate and meditation occur in most English versions of the Bible, but not very frequently.[17] However, the practice of meditation is quite widespread. It is at the heart of Hinduism and Buddhism in the Eastern traditions of religion, and it has a venerable

17. There are some twenty occurrences in the KJV. In the Old Testament the words used are *hāḡâ*, *śîaḥ*, and *śûaḥ*, or their cognates. Overall, there are some thirty occurrences of *hāḡâ* and its cognates. These are found in Gen. 24:63; Josh. 1:8; Pss. 1:2; 5:1; 19:14; 49:3 63:6; 77:12; 104:34; 119:15, 23, 48, 78, 97, 99, 148; Is. 33:18. These examples do not exhaust the use of these roots in the Old Testament, which adds to the difficulty of translation. In the New Testament, words translated as meditate are 1 Tim. 4:15 (*meletaō*). and Luke 21:14 (*promeletaō*).

history in Christianity.[18] The first question to be answered is the meaning of these words as they are used in the Bible.[19] The second question is whether the traditional ideas of meditation have any support in the Bible. Only then can we assess the modern practice of meditation, particularly as it has come to be used by Christians. The first occurrence of the words translated as *meditate* relates to Isaac (Gen. 24:63), but the NRSV gives the translation, 'Isaac went out in the evening to walk [instead of *meditate*] in the field.' A marginal note indicates that the meaning of the Hebrew word translated *walk* is uncertain.[20] However, the uncertainties seem to diminish when we look at the majority of occurrences. We find that, if meditation is the correct connotation, it is consistently provided with an object that requires some application of the mind and thought. Joshua is told to meditate on the book of the law (Josh. 1:8). The psalmists extol meditation on the law or the word of God (Pss. 1:2; 119:15, 23, 48, 78, 97, 99, 148). In Psalm 63:6–7 the psalmist meditates on God, 'for you have been my help'. In Psalm 77:12 the meditation is on all God's mighty work and deeds. Psalm 104 is summed up in verse 34 as a meditation on the creative work of God. There is some evidence that the words in question can also indicate speaking or even muttering, so that the suggestion is reasonable that the basic biblical sense of meditation is to recite the words of the law, or rehearse the mighty deeds of God. It is clear that the meaning in Luke 21:14 involves a consideration of the right answer to give under interrogation: 'So make up your minds not to prepare your defense in advance' (NRSV).

18. Ray C. Petry (ed.), *Late Medieval Mysticism*, Library of Christian Classics, Vol. XIII (London: SCM, 1957) gives a brief historical resumé of the background to contemplative mysticism, beginning with the pre-Christian Greek philosophers. In the early medieval period Augustine is named as one who wrote about such contemplative Christianity in Georgia Harkness, *Mysticism* (Nashville: Abingdon, 1973).

19. It is entirely possible that the meditation words in the Bible are used with a meaning quite different from the meaning given to them in modern thinking.

20. The ESV translates this word as *meditate*, but there is no indication from the context as to what Isaac was actually doing.

The evidence is clear; these words that are often translated as *meditate* refer to a rational use of the mind with the content of God's revelation as the object. However much it may include reflection on the significance of these words of God for our personal existence, they are first and foremost directed to careful evaluation of the content and meaning of God's words. The meditator is 'filled with thoughts of God's deeds and his will'.[21] We conclude that these words indicate a calling to mind, and even a recitation, of that which God has done for us and spoken to us. It is a rational exercise of the mind that issues in adoration and praise, and in a desire to live consistently with what God has done.

Is this what is usually meant today by meditation? It would seem not. It also appears that the medieval mystical tradition in Christianity is much more rational than the mysticism that seems to have come to us from the Eastern religions, although, as Ray Petry summarizes it, 'the highest form is an ecstasy without images, a ravishment of soul that defies ordinary means of knowing and doing'.[22] We may still find this kind of meditation and contemplative discipline among those who follow the style of life that was always suited to it, that of the monk or the hermit, but it is difficult to see this as in any real way representing the biblical concept of prayer.

The modern expression of meditation, even among Christians, is unashamedly syncretistic in that it acknowledges its debt to Hinduism and Buddhism.[23] In Western society it came into some prominence in the second half of the twentieth century with Transcendental Meditation and the phenomenon of the Hare Krishna sect. It became trendy when the Beatles went to India to visit the Maharishi. However, probably few practising Christians took much notice of Transcendental Meditation, nor of the Hare Krishna sect, except perhaps to try some of their interesting vegetarian

---

21. Article on *hāḡâ* in G. J. Botterweck and H. Ringgren, *Theological Dictionary of the Old Testament*, Vol. III, translated by John T. Willis, Geoffrey W. Bromiley and David E. Green (Grand Rapids: Eerdmans, 1978), pp. 321–4.

22. Ray C. Petry (ed.), *Late Medieval Mysticism*, Library of Christian Classics, Vol. XIII (London: SCM, 1957), p. 44.

23. Syncretism is the mixing of elements of other religions with one's own.

cooking. It was really part of the hippy scene and the growing movement for alternative lifestyles and New Age thinking rather than a serious movement within Christianity. However there is evidence that Christians are once again becoming more involved in the practice of meditation, but this time it seems to have more in common with Eastern religion than with the kind of medieval mystical and contemplative practices of the monasteries.

One example will suffice to illustrate the practice. In a religious television programme the British Benedictine monk Laurence Freeman was interviewed concerning his promotion of meditation among Christians.[24] Laurence Freeman has lectured around the world and written on the subject of meditation. He attributed his coming to the meditative practice through another monk who was his teacher. This monk, in turn, had learned the practice of meditation from an Indian swami (a Hindu religious teacher) in Malaysia. Freeman described meditation as contemplative prayer 'beyond words and images'. He rejected the notion that such a practice gave opportunity to the devil, because the Spirit of God indwells us. He advocated the use of a mantra, a word or phrase ('a sacred word') that is repeated over and over in order to help one 'leave the shallows and enter the depths of your own being'. The mantra helps one overcome distractions, particularly from thoughts about the past and the future, so that 'we can slip into the present moment'. Members of a meditation group that meet regularly at a Sydney city Anglican church spoke of the peace and joy that such meditation brings.[25] Freeman, in describing meditation, says it enables one to move from the head to the heart. This is a false distinction, since the heart, in biblical terms, includes the will and thinking along with the emotions.

I would not want to suggest, as some do, that this kind of activity

---

24. The monk, Laurence Freeman, was interviewed on the program *Compass*, broadcast by the Australian Broadcasting Corporation on Sunday, 20 October 2002.

25. One interviewee claimed that this meditation fulfilled the biblical injunction 'Be still, and know that I am God' (Ps. 46:10). The context does not really support this interpretation since, if anything, it invites consideration of the saving work of God and his Lordship over the nations.

is always fraught with spiritual danger, especially when practised in the context of Christian faith. It would, however, be idolatrous if it distracted us from the biblical practice of prayer. Without clear evidence, I certainly would not suggest that there are no psychological gains in sitting still and becoming aware of ourselves, relaxing and mentally unwinding. I would say, however, that this is not prayer in the biblical sense unless we address God with our minds. Prayer is not a going into our inner being. Self-examination and personal reflection do that, and these may then result in prayer. But the essence of prayer, as we have seen, is a conscious going out to our Father in heaven, through the mediation of the risen Christ. The Spirit within us does not have the primary role of taking us in, but of taking us out of ourselves to God.[26]

Should we pray for the dead?

Protestant Christians have always rejected the practice of Roman Catholics, and of some other religions, of praying for the dead. The reasons traditionally given for this stance include:

- The rejection of any idea of a second chance after death. After death comes the judgment (Heb. 9:27).
- Nothing we do or pray can change a person's state or status once they have died.
- There is no example or teaching in the Bible that would commend or support the practice.
- To pray for the righteous dead implies that their situation is uncertain rather than being secure in the presence of Christ. Our prayers can achieve nothing for them for they have reached the goal with Christ. Their final 'clothing' is certain (2 Cor. 5:1–8).[27]
- Prayers for the dead undermine the clarity of the doctrine of justification by faith on the grounds of Christ's perfect righteousness.

---

26. See Edmund P. Clowney, *Christian Meditation* (Leicester: Inter-Varsity Press, 1980).
27. Protestant funeral or memorial services traditionally use prayers of thanksgiving for the life of the departed, and pray for the bereaved.

Furthermore, Protestants reject the Roman Catholic doctrine of purgatory, upon which a huge structure, including prayers for the dead and prayers to Mary and the saints, is built. Catholicism provides little scriptural underpinning for a tradition that grows out of the whole reversal of grace and justification.[28] Rejection of the Reformation doctrine of justification by faith alone accompanied a view of grace that located it in the sacraments of the church. Justification was by grace alone in the sense that the grace of regeneration in baptism and through the other sacraments of the church led to sanctification. Sanctification, rather than being the fruit of justification, was seen as its cause. The Reformers rejected this understanding of grace and proclaimed that God justifies the ungodly on the basis of faith in the finished work of Christ.[29] They saw these Roman Catholic doctrines as undermining the whole sense of security for the believer and the assurance of salvation. Justification with its accompanying assurance, then, produces sanctification. By reversing this relationship, Catholicism left the believer in a state of uncertainty and requiring the cleansing of purgatory.[30] Prayers for the dead are specifically tied to this doctrine of purgatory, and thus they undermine the sufficiency of Christ's saving work for us.

---

28. Robert Ombres, OP, *Theology of Purgatory* (Dublin: Mercier, 1978), p. 21, suggests a number of scriptural proofs of purgatory. He goes on: 'It is unlikely that these texts would be tight enough as "proofs" for the whole truth of purgatory, and so it is better to see how purgatory emerges from a number of larger truths, and not overload a limited set of isolated texts.'
29. Calvin, *Institutes*, book III, chapter v, section 6: 'Therefore, we must cry out with the shouting not only of our own voices but of our throats and lungs that purgatory is a deadly fiction of Satan, which nullifies the cross of Christ, inflicts unbearable contempt upon God's mercy, and overturns and destroys our faith.'
30. Josef Neuner, SJ and Heinrich Roos, SJ, *The Teaching of the Catholic Church*, edited by Karl Rahner, SJ, (New York: Alba House, 1967), p. 414: 'Souls which depart this life without sin or punishment due to sin, go to eternal happiness . . . The soul which has temporal punishment still due goes to purgatory. The faithful can help the holy souls by prayer and good works.'

Conclusion

I want to conclude on a positive note. We have a great and a gracious God. His plan, a plan devised before the foundation of the world, is being worked out before our eyes. We see but a small part of it during our lives, yet we have all we need to know about its author, its origins, its course and its final outcome. We have this plainly set out in Holy Scripture. To have the assurance that we are caught up into this plan and actually participate in its outworking is blessing indeed. Some might think that God could conceivably have executed his will without using us as his agents in any way. While that seems theoretically possible, it would strike a blow at the significance of our union with Christ and the fellowship we have with God through him. God has chosen to glorify his name and character by allowing us to be involved actively, self-consciously and responsibly. The very nature of the gospel as the work of the incarnated Son of God requires that, in Christ, we become praying people. The dimension of prayer is perhaps one of the most astonishing aspects of God's plan, in that he allows redeemed sinners actually to ask him to do his gracious will. This is no cynical exercise giving us an illusion of being important when all the time we are being manipulated like clockwork toys. It is rather the gracious expression of his Fatherhood and of our beloved sonship. It is fellowship of the most profound nature. It is a foretaste of eternity with God. My words can never suffice to tell of the love of God towards us, and of the privilege we have as God's children in being enabled to call upon him with boldness and confidence. So, let Paul have the last word:

> And because you are sons, God has sent the Spirit of his Son into our hearts, crying, 'Abba! Father!'
>
> (Gal. 4:6)

Index of subjects and names

Index of Scripture references